Game on!

Andy Harvey-John Oakley

**A Teacher's
Resource Book
of Activities
for English
Language Learners**

Express Publishing

Contents

Introduction

Why will this book be useful to me?

Give us the tools and we'll finish the job.

This is a book of game-based activities for language teachers to use with students of all ages and levels, from beginner to advanced.

You will find 150 practical ready-to-use activities for pair, group, and class work which you can draw on and modify to enrich the learning experience for your students. The activities go beyond normal course book tasks, stimulate students' imaginations, get them involved in purposeful and enjoyable learning experiences, and strengthen their communicative language skills.

The activities, suitable for use at different stages of lessons and courses, can be used independently of a course book or to provide extra practice of specific language points and skills.

Game On! provides ideas and materials for developing, extending and consolidating student learning and competence in vocabulary, grammar and pronunciation, and helps students develop and improve their skills in speaking, listening, reading and writing.

Preparation time is minimal. Materials required are often little more than pencil and paper. Many materials are provided in photocopiable form or are produced by the students themselves.

Why do we need games?

The play's the thing.

Game playing is a natural human activity, appealing to people of all ages. Games provide a framework within which to explore possibilities, use knowledge, develop abilities and relate meaningfully with others while having fun.

Games motivate, challenge and focus; they also encourage co-operation as well as competition while players work towards a goal.

In the language learning classroom, games allow students to practise language intensively and use it creatively. The teacher can step out of the spotlight and concentrate on helping students as they proceed with the games in pairs or groups. Such activities are highly efficient. With a class of twenty students, a ten-minute class discussion can only yield ten minutes of English with most students having little opportunity to participate, as they have to speak one by one. The same activity, with students working in pairs, results in a hundred minutes of spoken language with every student involved.

How can I use this book?

Give a man a fish and you feed him for a day.
Teach a man to fish and you feed him for life.

We suggest you start by skimming through the book to get a general idea of the type of material presented. You can then select more specifically for your students' needs and interests. An underlying idea of this book, however, is to encourage you and your students to adapt the activities and to generate your own content within the activity frameworks you find here.

Why get students involved in preparing materials?

Many hands make light work.

The more students are involved in the development and the progression of an activity, the more motivated they are and the more successful the outcome is likely to be. Students appreciate being involved; it gives them a chance to demonstrate what they know and contribute their own ideas to classroom activities.

- Students interact in the target language as they co-operate to produce materials
- Materials produced are linguistically tuned to the students' level
- Material content reflects students' interests
- Students learn to become more responsible for their own learning
- The teacher has more freedom and opportunity to focus on individual learners
- Student-produced materials can be used with other classes

What will I find in this book?

Variety is the spice of life.

Six Sections:

> Starters & Fillers
> Talking Together
> Vocabulary
> Grammar
> Pronunciation [sounds, rhythm & intonation]
> Texts

- Games within each section are arranged by level. Most games can also be used with other levels.
- Each game tells you what the focus is, the timing, the materials you will need and whether it is best played in pairs, groups or as a class.
- Games have step by step procedures, examples and, where required, photocopiable cards and boards.
- Activities require students to interact. Sometimes the language produced will be limited by the activity, at other times it will be totally free.
- *The Writing on the Wall (page 6),* offers 10 ideas you might consider on how to use the walls of your classroom more effectively to create a dynamic and interesting physical environment.

Starters & Fillers

Good things come in small packages.

These short activities are particularly useful for starting off a lesson, using spare time constructively, or providing extension activities for particular language points. Many of them involve students being physically or imaginatively active.

Talking Together

It's good to talk.

In conversation we use whatever resources we have to initiate, maintain and respond to messages appropriately.
These activities will encourage students to use the English they know in challenging and motivating tasks. The emphasis here is on developing fluency in natural speech activities.

Vocabulary

A rose by any other name would smell as sweet.

The labels we give objects and ideas are pretty much arbitrary but they have certain associations, collocations, connotations, sounds, spellings and relations with each other. The activities here explore such issues, first focusing on spelling, then word, and finally lexical phrases.

Grammar

Me Tarzan, you Jane!

With vocabulary you can say things, but with grammar you can say things more effectively.
We select words and these associate with others and change in different ways according to the context of the communication. e.g. Is it a past experience? Is it hypothetical? Am I making a proposal?
These activities focus on the combinatorial system of English – the system whereby words are selected and put together to produce a message.

Pronunciation

It's not what you say but the way that you say it.

A spoken message can be obscured if it is unclear or ambiguous. The utterance: "*I want to leave there.*" might be heard as: "*I went to live there.*" Not quite the same thing.
The activities in this section are designed to help learners improve their verbal communication by focusing on individual sounds, word stress, rhythm and intonation patterns.

Texts

What use is a book without pictures?

Every time we read, write or listen to something, we are using our imagination to provide the pictures to accompany the text we are dealing with. Here we are concerned with texts and ways to use them in the English class.

Every text has a purpose and is intended to produce a response, which is why most of the ideas you find here involve interaction.

This section starts with songs, poems and stories for young learners as they are familiar with such texts in their mother tongue culture. At higher levels, there are a variety of activities for exploiting different types of text.

The writing on the wall.

1 Graffiti board

Have extra boards (black/white) or notice boards covered with large sheets of paper around the class and lots of coloured chalk/felt markers/pencils available.

During breaks and before and after class, students write up whatever they want in English (words, lines from songs, mottoes, slogans, ads they've seen, etc). The board is only cleaned or sheets of paper removed when it is full.

2 Survey charts

Projects/challenges to do each week/month. Make charts and stick/draw them on the wall/board. Students tick the columns they've done. Choose a time for students to talk about where, why, when, and with whom they did it.

e.g. *In the last week who has...?*

Name	Had a dream	Been to the cinema	Gone to bed after 12	Read a new book
John		✓		
Anne	✓			
Maria				
Andy	✓			

3 Cut-outs

Pictures are cut out from magazines (perhaps on themes) and stuck on a wall/board. e.g. famous people, sports, animals, etc. Students write a small paragraph about the picture/subject on a card or sheet of paper and stick it around the picture.

Alternatively, each wall is designated a different colour. Students find, cut out and bring in pictures of various items in these colours. Students write one or two sentences on a card about the item and stick it next to the picture.

4 Plasticine monsters

Students make plasticine monsters or funny animals to display on a shelf and write a short biography about them.

5 Food shelf/label collage

Students bring in various food packets/tins or labels and write a description of them. e.g. where they are from, what they look like, taste like, how they are cooked, what they are eaten with etc.

6 Family tree

Students draw their family tree and write a few sentences about the people in it.

7 Word fields

Pictures and lexical items are added around a central word/theme. e.g. Environment, sports, clothes, etc.

8 Idiom corner

Write up idiomatic expressions/proverbs in English and their equivalent (if there is) in the students' mother tongue or from the mother tongue to English.

9 Top of the pops

Students compile a top twenty list of favourite songs in English and write them on the wall/board. Each one has a number. The numbers are written on cards and one is drawn out of a bag/hat. The chosen song is the one to be played in class. The student who has the song brings it in on CD or cassette with the lyrics (if possible). The words can be written up next to the song title on the wall.

10 Our world

Stick a big colourful map of your country or the world on the wall. Build up information about different places by getting students to write facts on small cards which are stuck on/by the map. They could start with capital cities, famous landmarks, or interesting facts they find out or hear in the news. Students could also focus on a different region or country each month.

Feet on the Ground

Some practical points to get the most out of the games in this book.

BEFORE PLAYING

Look through the book with colleagues and decide where the games could fit in with the course you are teaching and materials you are using.

Decide whether a game could be altered or adapted to suit your aims and the students' needs. (e.g. enlarging photocopiable material or producing more cards)

Think of how the materials for the games could be produced by the students.

Many games require counters and/or spinners (as an alternative to dice). There is a picture of an easy to make spinner using a pencil and a piece of cardboard on p. 6. Students spin the pencil and whatever side of the hexagon lands on the table is the number that will be used. Students can make their own counters from a variety of small objects, coloured cards or plasticine.

Share the tasks of photocopying and cutting with the students. Make the boards and cards more durable by sticking them onto cardboard and laminating them if possible.

File the materials appropriately and accessibly. (e.g. keep letter tiles in an envelope/box)

Arrange seating and tables so it is easy for interaction to take place and for you to move around the classroom.

Vary groupings so students don't always speak with the same people.

Ensure students know what they are supposed to do in each game - with whom, in what order, for how long and to what end.

You may want to use more than one of the following strategies:

- **Demonstration**

Whenever possible, show the students what they have to do. For simple pair work activities, the teacher can first work through a task with one student, then get one pair to carry out all or part of the task in front of the rest of the class. Once you are sure that all the students know what they have to do, then all pairs can work on the task simultaneously.

- **Oral instructions in L1**

This is perhaps most suitable when working with Young Learners and/or beginners. There is no point in trying to give instructions in the target language if this is going to take up most of the lesson time. Obviously, such a technique will not work if the class is of a multi-lingual background.

- **Oral instructions in English**

This encourages the students to listen to the language they are learning. Also, students will be more likely to think in English as they work out what they have to do and so are more likely to ask any questions they may have using the target language.

- **Written instructions**

Some games may have fairly complicated rules and instructions. In such cases it may be better to provide a set of written instructions – thus providing students with a real reading comprehension task to carry out as well.

Get students to repeat the rules and aims to check that they have got the idea.

WHILE PLAYING

Be flexible in the timing and rules of the various activities.

Move around the classroom helping, participating, monitoring, and encouraging equal participation. You might note down language errors students make which you can work on with them at a later time.

Pairs or groups playing a game will not all finish an activity at the same time unless you set a time limit, so have something to occupy those who complete the task while others are still playing.

Some teachers find playing unobtrusive background music helps create an atmosphere conducive to speaking together.

AFTER PLAYING

After each game, encourage feedback from the students.

Share with colleagues how the games went with your classes and how you might customise them to better meet your students' needs.

Store the materials for re-use.

We hope you find these activities enrich your work.

Have fun!

1 Starters and Fillers

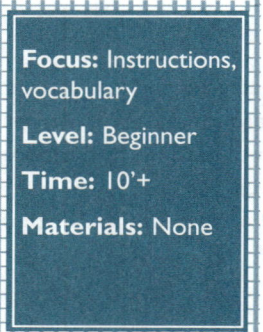

1 Simon Says
(Class)

Focus: Instructions, vocabulary

Level: Beginner

Time: 10'+

Materials: None

Procedure:

Revise common action verbs if needed.
Have students push their desks back and stand in a circle in the middle of the room.
Ask students to perform an action – saying: *'Simon says …'* before the action.
e.g. *'Simon says touch your nose.'*
If Simon tells them to do it, then they perform the action.
If, however, they are told to perform an action without hearing the words: *'Simon says …'*
e.g. *'Touch your nose.'* - they shouldn't do it.
If a student performs an action without hearing *'Simon says …'*, that student is out and takes over the role of Simon. The game continues until there is only one student left.

Sample instructions:

Touch something red
Touch your toes
Point to me
Stand up
Sit down
Stand on one leg

Tickle the person on your right
Stretch as far as you can
Close your eyes
Laugh
Go to sleep
Clap your hands

2 Drawback
(Pairs)

Focus: Spelling, guessing

Level: Beginner

Time: 5'+

Materials: None

Procedure:

Students work in pairs.
Student A draws a letter [A], a word [HELLO], or a little picture [SUN, BOAT, HOUSE] on their partner's back with their finger.
Student B has to guess what has been sketched. If student B can't guess, they can ask for student A to repeat the action.

With higher levels, students can draw short phrases or messages.

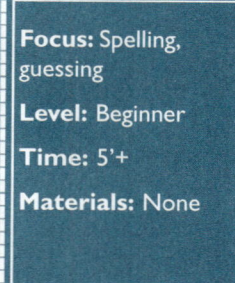

Slap, Clap, Click, Click.
(Class)

Focus: Learning names, story telling, concentration

Level: Beginner - Pre-intermediate

Time: 10'+

Materials: None

Procedure:

Have students push their desks back and sit in a circle.

Tell the students to put their hands out and on your signal - slap their thighs with both hands, then clap their hands, then click their fingers - first right hand, then left. The class must do this all together at the same time and then keep the rhythm going.

 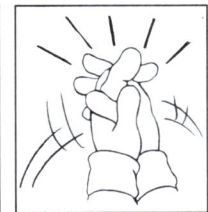  

The first student [e.g. John] on the right hand click says his name and on the 2nd click the name of the person to his left [e.g. Maria]. Keeping the rhythm going, Maria now says *'Maria'* on the right hand click, then the next person's name – *'Ahmed'* – on the left hand click. This goes on round the circle as shown by the black arrows.

e.g. John: slap, clap, *John, Maria.*
     Maria: slap, clap, *Maria, Ahmed.*
     Ahmed: slap, clap, *Ahmed, Stan.*

After this first round, the first student (John) says his name on the right hand click and then says the name of anybody else in the class on the 2nd click. That student must be alert to say their name after the usual SLAP, CLAP, and on the 2nd click say the name of another student.

The game continues in this way as shown by the blue arrows.

e.g. John: slap, clap, *John, Stan.*
     Stan: slap, clap, *Stan, Ian.*

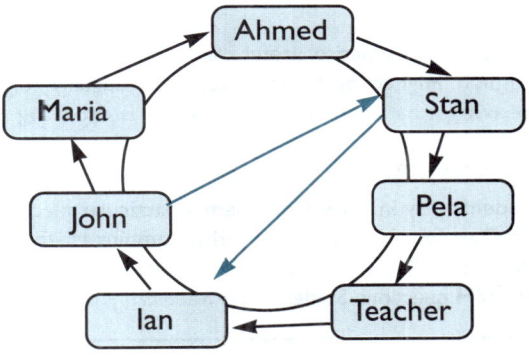

A student who does not respond or responds incorrectly is 'out', but stays in the circle and continues to keep the rhythm going. The student next to the one who has just become 'out' continues the game. Students have to remember who is out of the game. If by mistake a student, e.g. John says, *"John, Ahmed"* and Ahmed is already out of the game, then John drops out too.

The game ends when half the students are out.

The game can then be played again, with a different focus (see below).

Variation 1:

The game can be played with words belonging to the same lexical field or numbers to revise vocabulary.

e.g. the letter **C** – cap, car...car, cat...cat, cow...
    Animals   – dog, cat...cat, cow...cow, goat...goat, kangaroo...kangaroo, panda...
    Numbers   – One, two ... two, three ...three, four ...
                  – three, six ... six, nine ... nine twelve ...

In the above variation, students have to repeat the last word said by the previous student before they say their new word.

Variation 2:

Student A says two words, one on each click to start a story. Student B continues the story, by saying a word on each click. This goes on around the circle until no one can continue.

e.g. Story Telling - *One day... I went... to school... and I... found that... my teacher... was away... so I...,* etc

Circle Stamp
4 (Class)

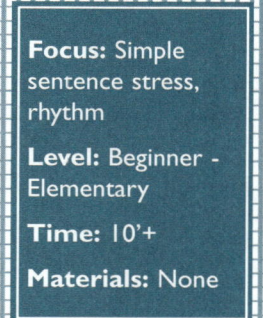

☞ **Pointer:**

To help students with the stress and rhythm of English it is useful to exaggerate such features.

Focus: Simple sentence stress, rhythm

Level: Beginner - Elementary

Time: 10'+

Materials: None

Procedure:

Have students push their desks back and put their chairs in a circle.

Students stamp their feet: left, right, left, right to get a rhythm going. As they stamp, students count **1, 2, 3, 4** to the rhythm. This rhythm doesn't stop.

Think of simple phrases such as: **What's** your **name? My** name's **Pedro.** Clap the rhythm of these phrases - one clap for each syllable. Then say each phrase and get the class to repeat it while you continue to clap the rhythm.

e.g.   Clap   clap   clap

      What's your **name?**

      1   **2**   **3**   **4**

      My   name's   **Pedro.**

For longer sentences slow the rhythm down as there will be more syllables between the stresses. The basic 4/4 stamping rhythm must not change.

e.g.   **What** would you like to **do** tonight?

      1   **2**   **3**   **4**

      I'd **like** to go and **see** a play.

Lower levels: practise useful classroom language, e. g. **open** your **books, look** at the **board, talk** to your **partner, speak** in **English.** Higher levels: more complex language, e.g. Students describe what is happening in a picture: The **girl** in the corner is **wearing** a hat. The **man** with the suit is **crossing** the road.

Extension:

Students play in pairs. Give them a particular piece of language to practice.

e.g. **Can** for ability. Pairs start the stamping rhythm. Student A: **Can** you **swim?** Student B: **Yes, I can. / No, I can't.**

Student A: **Can** you ride a **bike?**   etc

e.g. **WH** questions. Student A: **Where** can you **swim?** Student B: **In the sea.** Student A: **Where** can you **drive?** Student **B:On** the road.

Word Box
5 (Class)

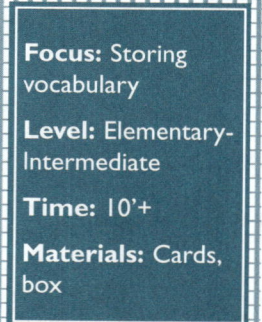

Focus: Storing vocabulary

Level: Elementary-Intermediate

Time: 10'+

Materials: Cards, box

Procedure:

At the end of each week, students pick new vocabulary from their course books and note books which they write on cards and put in a box kept handy in the classroom.

The cards can be colour-coded according to parts of speech or topic area.

Allocate a time to revise these items. Students come up, choose a card and give a definition, translation, opposite, mime or synonym and ask the class to guess the word.

Variation (for collocations):

Students play in groups of three.

Three boxes are provided - one for verbs/adjectives, another for prepositions and a third for nouns.

The cards are divided equally among the students. The students match them to make collocations.

e.g. INTERESTED + IN, MAKE + INQUIRY

Students then use the collocations to form sentences and read them out to the class. The one to use all of their cards is the winner.

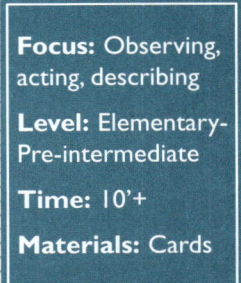

Mirror Image
(Pairs)

Photocopiable Material: pp. 132-133

Focus: Observing, acting, describing

Level: Elementary-Pre-intermediate

Time: 10'+

Materials: Cards

Procedure:

Students play in pairs, facing each other. Photocopy and give each pair a mime card. Student A begins the mime and student B mirrors every action student A performs as closely as possible. Pairs practise together and then each pair performs their mimes in front of the class. Students write down what they think the action is.
Each correct guess gets a point. The student with the most points is the winner.

Sample Cards:

Brushing your teeth	Making a pizza	Watching a horror film	Making a cake	Ironing a shirt	Planting a small tree
Making a cup of tea	Washing the dishes	Washing clothes by hand	Standing in a queue for a long time	Watching an exciting football match	Frying eggs

---

Slow Motion
(Class)

Photocopiable Material: pp. 132-133

> ☞ **Pointer:**
>
> As in Tai Chi, where movements are slow and fluid, students perform actions slowly and continuously.

Focus: Following instructions, observing

Level: Elementary

Time: 10'+

Materials: Cards

Procedure:

Have students push their desks back and sit in a circle.
Start with simple actions for the whole class to do. e.g Stand up. Pick up your books and put them in your bag. Shake hands with the person on your right. Raise your left knee as high as it will go...and raise your right arm as high as you can. Now, bring them both down.
Give each student a card with a different action on it. Students take it in turns to perform the actions in front of the class.
e.g. preparing, eating and clearing away breakfast
While the student is miming the action, the others note down exactly what that person is doing or provide a commentary: 'You're preparing breakfast... you're eating cereal...'

Alternative:

Students note down what the mimer missed out. e.g. 'You forgot to clear away the dishes.'

Sample Cards:

Getting dressed	Cooking a meal	Making a brick wall	Making a cup of tea	Putting up a tent

What's my line?
(Groups)

Photocopiable Material: p. 134

Focus: Jobs, actions

Level: Elementary-Pre-intermediate

Time: 10'+

Materials: Cards

Procedure:

Divide the class into two groups.

Students write down various types of jobs on cards.

Collect and shuffle the cards. Place them face down on a desk at the front of the classroom.

A member of group A picks up the first card and mimes that job for their group to guess.

Each group has 3 guesses.

If they guess correctly, they keep the card. If they don't, group B can guess and take the card.

Then a member from group B mimes for their team.

The winning team is the one with the most cards at the end of the game.

Instead of jobs, the cards can be of different activities.

e.g. eating spaghetti, taking the dog for a walk, etc

Sample Cards:

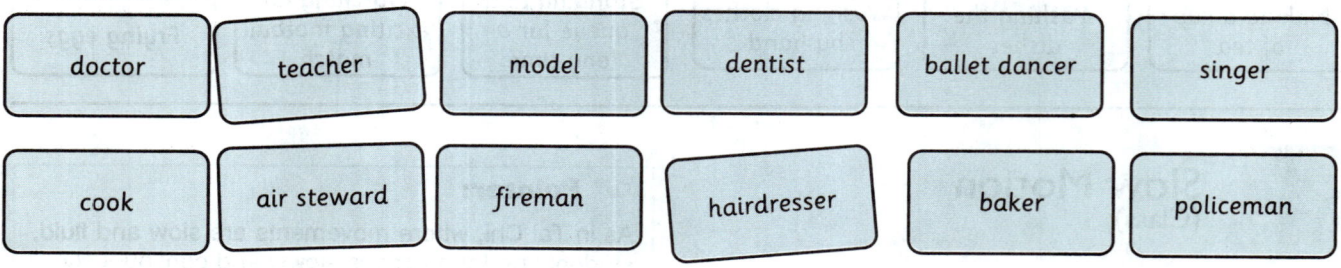

doctor | teacher | model | dentist | ballet dancer | singer

cook | air steward | fireman | hairdresser | baker | policeman

Just imagine ...
(Groups)

Focus: Listening, describing, writing

Level: Elementary-Pre-intermediate

Time: 10'+

Materials: Music

Procedure:

Divide the class into two groups.

Students close their eyes and listen to a piece of instrumental music with the lights off/dimmed.

Ask the students to concentrate on the music and the feelings and images it brings to mind.

Stop the music after a few minutes.

Have the students draw or write down what they felt or thought of while listening to the music.

Students share their impressions with the rest of their group and try to find another student who had similar impressions.

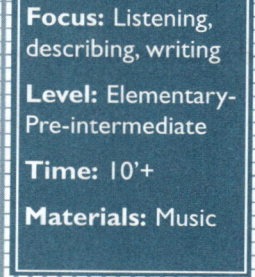

Gestures
(Class)

10

Photocopiable Material: p. 135

Procedure:

Students take it in turns to pick up a card and mime a gesture/facial expression.
The class guesses what they think the gesture/facial expression is.
The first student to guess correctly wins a toothpick and it is now their turn to play.
The winner is the student who has collected the most toothpicks when the time is up.

Start off with well-known gestures or expressions, then players can make up their own.

Focus: Gestures, facial expressions, feelings

Level: Elementary-Pre-intermediate

Time: 10' +

Materials: Cards, toothpicks

Sample Cards:

frightened | bored | Keep quiet! | Don't move! | tired | cold

sad | What's the time? | surprised | Come here. | hungry | sleepy

---

What am I doing?
(Class)

11

Procedure:

Have students face the back of the classroom so they can't see you.
Use objects to make various noises.
e.g. bounce a ball, sharpen a pencil, write on the board, pick up some keys, tear a piece of paper or cough, sneeze, etc.
After 5 actions, students open their eyes and write down the actions in the order they think they were done. Each student passes their paper to the student on their right.
Read out the actions in the right order and students mark the paper in front of them.

Focus: Listening, recognising sounds

Level: Elementary

Time: 10'+

Materials: Objects which make noise

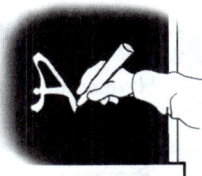

Pick one of the students who had all 5 actions in the right order to repeat the game with different noises.

If I were an animal...
12 (Groups)

Focus: Asking questions

Level: Elementary-Pre-intermediate

Time: 10'+

Materials: Pencil, paper, toothpicks,

Procedure:

Divide the class into two groups.
Give each student three toothpicks.
Ask students to close their eyes and imagine: *If they were an animal, what would they be?*
After 10 seconds students open their eyes and write down the name of the animal, making sure not to show it to the other members of their group.
Student A begins by asking: *'What animal am I?'*
The group has a maximum of ten 'yes/no' questions they can ask to identify the animal.

e.g. *Do you have a tail?*   *Do you eat other animals?*   *Can you swim?*
Do you have four legs?   *Do you live in Asia?*   *Can you climb trees?*
Are you bigger than I am?   *Do you have stripes?*
Are you a tiger?

Each time a student gets a 'yes' answer, they get an extra toothpick. If a student thinks they know what the animal is and names it and the answer is wrong, they lose a toothpick.
If a student guesses the animal correctly, they get a toothpick. If nobody identifies the animal after ten questions, student A gives a clue and the group can ask five more questions.
If students have still not identified the animal, student A gets a toothpick and play goes to the next student in the group.
The winner is the student with the most toothpicks after everyone has had a turn.
Students can play the game using other topics. e.g. colours, drinks, places, plants, foods etc

On the train
13 (Class)

Photocopiable Material: p. 136

Focus: Feelings

Level: Elementary-Pre-intermediate

Time: 10'+

Materials: Cards

Procedure:

Have students make a 'train' at the front of the class with the chairs facing each other.
Photocopy or prepare cards with different feelings on them and place them at the front of the class.
Select a number of students to be 'passengers'.
'Passengers' pick a card from the pile which tells them how they are feeling.
e.g. bored, in a hurry, worried, sick, irritated, happy, uncomfortable, depressed, sad, hot, cold, scared, etc.
The adjectives may be written on the board as well.
The 'watchers' write down the names of the 'passengers' in a list. 'Passengers' wait on the platform. The train arrives and they get on and sit down. The train starts and the 'watchers' have 30 seconds to guess how each of the 'passengers' feels and write it next to their name. e.g. James-bored, Kate-uncomfortable
The 'watchers' take it in turns to ask the passengers questions and tick off the ones they got correct.
   e.g. *'James, did you feel bored?'*   *'Kate, were you uncomfortable?'*
The 'passengers' then switch places with the 'watchers' who pick different cards.

Sample Cards:

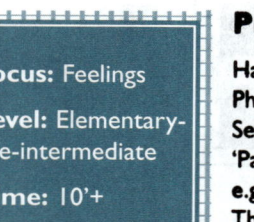

| bored | worried | happy | scared | cold |

14 Funny Walks
(Groups)

Photocopiable Material: p. 137

> ☞ **Pointer:**
> Play some non-intrusive instrumental music in the background.

Focus: Guessing types of people

Level: Elementary-Pre-intermediate

Time: 10'+

Materials: Cards, pencil, paper

Procedure:

Divide the class into two groups.

Have the students push their desks back and stand in a circle.

Photocopy or prepare role cards and place them on a desk at the front of the room.

Group A chooses role cards from the pile, reads them and places them on the bottom of the pile.

Group A now walks around the classroom in that role for one minute.

Group B watches and tries to guess what type of person each 'walker' is miming.

Group B writes a description of the type of person next to the name of the 'walker' on a piece of paper.

e.g. John - a policeman   Maria - an old man

The student with the most correct matches win.

The groups now switch roles.

Sample Cards:

a busy businessman

someone carrying heavy shopping

a policeman on patrol

a clown

a two year old

an army officer

a famous singer

an old man

15 Find the word
(Groups)

Focus: Guessing words from clues

Level: Elementary-Pre-intermediate

Time: 10'+

Materials: None

Procedure:

Divide the class into two groups.

A student from group A goes to the front of the class and sits with their back to the board, facing the class.

A member of group B writes a word on the board. The members of group A call out words, one at a time, to help the student at the front guess the word written on the board.

After each word is called out, the student makes a guess. If the student can guess the word in 30 seconds or 5 clues, group A gets a point. If it is not correct, group A gives another clue.

Now it is group B's turn to guess a word written on the board by group A.

e.g.   A member of group B writes the word WATER on the board.

     Group A: *wet*
     Guessing student: *sea*
     Group A: *drink*
     Guessing student: *tea*
     Group A: *river*
     Guessing student: *water!*

Fawlty Towers
(Groups)

16

Photocopiable Material: p. 138

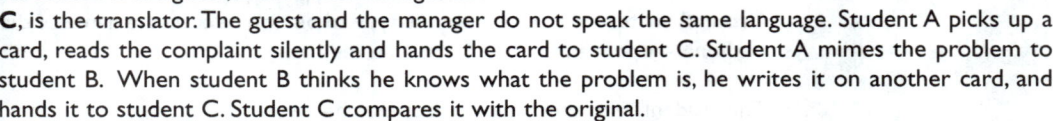

Focus: Communicating non-verbally

Level: Elementary-Intermediate

Time: 10'+

Materials: Cards

Procedure:

Students play in groups of three.

Each group writes three cards with a problem that a guest in a hotel might complain about on each one. Groups pass their cards to another group.

Student **A** is the guest, **B** the hotel manager and **C**, is the translator. The guest and the manager do not speak the same language. Student A picks up a card, reads the complaint silently and hands the card to student C. Student A mimes the problem to student B. When student B thinks he knows what the problem is, he writes it on another card, and hands it to student C. Student C compares it with the original.

If they match, student B gets a point. Students switch roles and play with a different problem card.

Sample Cards:

There's no hot water.	The shower doesn't work.	There is a nasty smell in the room.	The room is freezing.	The lift is broken.
The bathroom mirror is broken.	I want a double, not two single beds.	You have given me the wrong key.	The telephone does not work.	There is no shampoo.

Manchester
(Groups)

17

Focus: Word fnding, spelling

Level: Elementary-Intermediate

Time: 10'+

Materials: Pencil, paper

Procedure:

Divide the class into two groups.

Students try to make as many words as they can from a given start word.

For each word made, letters can only be used as many times as they occur in the start word.

e.g. MANCHESTER: man, chest, ten, team, chat, rat, tree, meant, tram, match, etc

The group who comes up with the greatest number of words in a given time is the winner.

Possible start words on the theme of places:
ALEXANDRIA, NEWCASTLE, MELBOURNE, MONTEVIDEO, BUDAPEST, MARAKESH

Buzz
(Class)

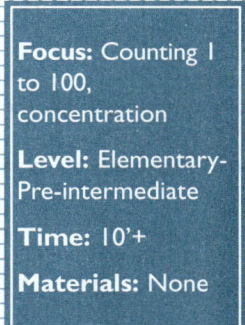

Focus: Counting 1 to 100, concentration

Level: Elementary-Pre-intermediate

Time: 10'+

Materials: None

Procedure:

Have students push their desks back and sit in a circle.
Choose a number to be the buzz number – e.g. 5
Student A starts off by saying 'one', student B says 'two' and so on until they come to a student whose number is a buzz number [or multiple of it, 10, 15, 20 …].
That student, instead of saying what their number would be (e.g.: 5), says 'buzz'.
If they do not say 'buzz', but 'five', they are out of the game.
The counting goes on until 100 and should be rapid.

Variation:

Students can choose to say 'beep' instead of 'buzz'. If they say 'beep', the direction of play changes from clockwise to anti-clockwise.

Variation for high level groups:

Choose 2 numbers [say 3 &7]. 3 is a buzz number, 7 is a beep number.

e.g.	S1: 1	S2: 2	S3: BUZZ	S4: 4	S5: 5	S6: BUZZ
	S7: BEEP	S8: 8	S9: BUZZ	S10: 10	S1: 11	S2: BUZZ
	S3: 13	S4: BEEP	S5: BUZZ	S6: 16	S7: 17	S8: BUZZ
	S9: 19	S10: 20	S1: BUZZ, BEEP			

Pass the ball
(Class)

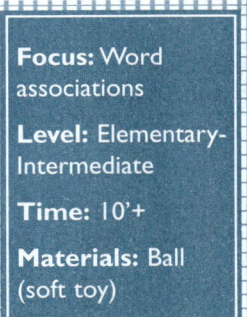

Focus: Word associations

Level: Elementary-Intermediate

Time: 10'+

Materials: Ball (soft toy)

Procedure:

Have students push their desks back and sit in a circle.
To start the game, throw a ball (bean bag or cuddly toy) to student A. As you throw say a word. Student A then throws the ball to another student and says a word that begins with the same letter. This continues around the circle. If a student can't think of a word, repeats a word already said or hesitates more than 5 seconds, that student loses a point. The next student then continues the game with a new word.

e.g. Teacher: *car*
    Student A: *coat*
    Student B: *cup*
    Student C: (can't think of an answer, so loses a point)
    Student D: *fox*

The winner is the student who has lost the fewest points at the end of the game.

Variations:

Words beginning with the last letter of the previous word. e.g. yellow, whale, egg, green, nest etc.
Word Associations/Opposites: e.g. day, night, sleep, dream, remember etc.

Surveys
(Class)

Photocopiable Material: p. 139

Focus: Finding out information

Level: Pre-intermediate - Intermediate

Time: 10'+

Materials: Questionnaire

Procedure:

Photocopy and hand out the questionnaire to the students.

Students ask each other yes/no questions. If they get a no answer, they move on and ask another student.

If they get a yes answer, they write that person's name on the form and ask a follow up question to get more information.

e.g. Martin: *'Ahmed, have you been abroad?'*
Ahmed: *'No, I haven't.'*
Martin: *'Peter. Have you been abroad?'*
Peter: *'Yes. I have.'*
Martin: *'Where have you been?'*
Peter: *'I've been to Russia.'*

Find someone who...	Name	More information
has got a brother. has eggs for breakfast. has been abroad. rides a bicycle. lives in your street/area.	Sally Peter	scrambled Russia

Allow 5 minutes for the students to get as much information as they can.

Call out a student's name, and the rest of the students take it in turns to say what they have learned about that student.

Extension:

Students write their own questionnaires.

Imagination
(Groups)

☞ **Pointer:**

Not all games have to be competitive or scored. The fun can come from simply doing and sharing.

Focus: Imagining, writing, speaking

Level: Pre-intermediate - Intermediate

Time: 10'+

Materials: Pencil, paper

Procedure:

Students play in groups of three.
Ask students to close their eyes and imagine they are looking at a lighted candle.
Ask them to think of a colour they can see in the flame and to imagine as many things as they can that are that colour, including personal possessions, memories and associations.
Ask students to open their eyes and write down what they thought of.

In groups they share with each other what they remember.

e.g. *'When I thought of white, I thought of snow, confetti, and my white Persian cat; long robes and fluffy white clouds.'*

Why?
22 (Class)

Photocopiable Material: p. 140

Focus: Finding out information
Level: Intermediate
Time: 10'+
Materials: Cards

Procedure:

Students write different questions on cards to which they would like to know the answer.

Collect the cards, shuffle them and place them face down at the front of the class.

Student A picks a card and reads the question to the class. Students take it in turns to answer the question. The class votes on who gave the best answer and that student gets the card.

The winner is the student with the most cards.

Sample cards:

Why is the sky blue?

Why does the sea have waves?

Why do we get colds?

Why do letters in a mirror go backwards but not upside down?

Why do the British drive on the left side of the road?

Why is the sea salty?

Why are stop signs and fire engines red?

Why can't penguins fly?

Tell me a story
23 (Class)

☞ **Pointer:**

Place a time limit on how long each group has to guess the story so it doesn't drag on.

Focus: Writing stories, miming
Level: Intermediate
Time: 15'+
Materials: Pencil, paper

Procedure:

Divide the class into two groups.

Each group writes a story (short paragraph), in which a lot of action takes place.

Group A chooses one student to mime their story, phrase by phrase. Group B has to call out what they think is happening.

Group A gives the thumbs up sign if what is said is correct or the thumbs down sign if it is incorrect.

e.g. Group A writes:

It was raining. I went out for a walk and I saw a wolf. I was scared. I started running but I fell down. Suddenly Tarzan appeared and hit the wolf on the nose. I was so relieved. I thanked Tarzan and asked him where Jane was. He laughed and said nothing. He couldn't understand me.

Group B now mimes their story.

Word Pyramids
(Groups)

Photocopiable Material: pp. 229-231

Focus: Spelling, vocabulary

Level: Intermediate

Time: 10'+

Materials: Pencil, paper, letter tiles

Procedure:

Students play in groups of three.
Give each group a bag/envelope of letter tiles, which contains the letters of the alphabet except: C, J, K, P, Q, U, V, X, Y, Z.

One student takes a letter from the bag and puts it down on the desk for their group to see. The rest of the letters are placed on the desk face up.
Student A has to pick a letter to add to the start letter to make a word.
Student B then adds a third letter to make another word.
The letters can be added at the beginning or end of the previous word.
Letters can also be rearranged as long as none are removed.
The winning group is the one which comes up with the longest word.

e.g.

A
AT
ATE
HATE
WHEAT
THAWED

In this example, W is added to the word 'HATE' to make 'WHEAT'. This involves changing the letter order.
If a student cannot proceed, they can change one letter of the last word down to make a new word.
e.g. change the W in THAWED for L to make HALTED - keeping the same number of letters in the new word.

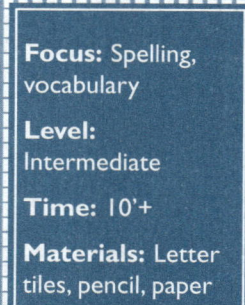

Use them both
(Groups)

Photocopiable Material: p.p. 229-231

Focus: Spelling, vocabulary

Level: Intermediate

Time: 10'+

Materials: Letter tiles, pencil, paper

Procedure:

Students play in groups of three.
Give each group 25 letter tiles which they place face down on the desk.
One student chooses 2 letter tiles and turns them over.
The group has one minute to write down as many words starting/containing these letters as they can.

e.g. letters picked are O and C
     Possible words: occur, occasion, court, code, colour, clock, etc.

The winner is the group with the most words made from their start letters.
Groups then pick two new letter tiles and play again.

Word to Word
(Groups)

Photocopiable Material: p. 141

Focus: Spelling, vocabulary

Level: Intermediate

Time: 10'+

Materials: Cards

Procedure:

Students play in groups of three.
Cards with a start and finish word are placed face down in a pile.
A student from each group picks a card.
Students have to change the start word, one letter at a time, to get to the final word.
Each time a letter is changed it must form a new word.

The group who gets to the finish word first or in the fewest moves wins.

Examples:

BOY to MAN: [boy – bay – may – man]
GOLD to BOOT [gold – good – food - foot – boot]
HATE to LOVE: [hate – late – gate – gave – wave – wove – love]

Sample Cards:

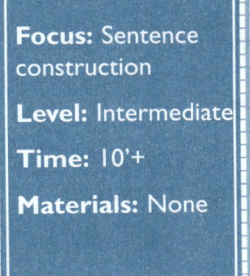

No E
(Pairs)

Focus: Sentence construction

Level: Intermediate

Time: 10'+

Materials: None

Procedure:

Students play in pairs.

Set a time limit (e.g. one minute)
Students have to write a sentence in which a certain letter is not allowed. e.g. the letter e

e.g. Nobody knows what I want to do with my big car.
You must study hard if you want to pass your finals.
I cannot put such things in this box so I'm told.

The longest sentence which makes some kind of sense wins.

 **28** # Anagrams
(Groups)

Photocopiable Material: p. 142

Focus: Spelling, word play

Level: Intermediate

Time: 10'+

Materials: Cards

Procedure:

Students play in groups of three.
Prepare and give each group 5 word cards. The word on each card must make at least one anagram.
Groups try to find the anagram(s) by using all the letters of the word on the card.

e.g. RATS - STAR or ARTS

The first group to find an anagram for each of their cards wins.

Sample Cards:

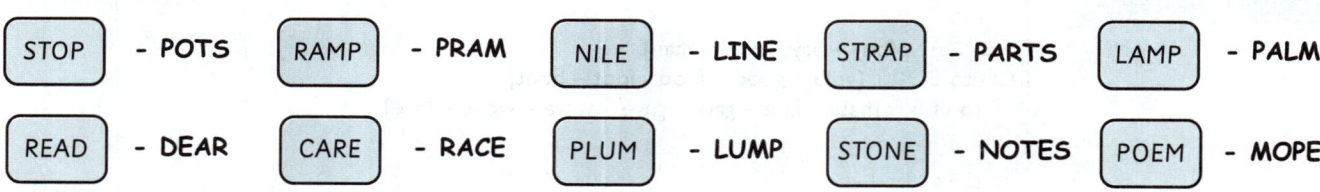

STOP - POTS   RAMP - PRAM   NILE - LINE   STRAP - PARTS   LAMP - PALM

READ - DEAR   CARE - RACE   PLUM - LUMP   STONE - NOTES   POEM - MOPE

Alternative:

Clues could be given on the cards to help.

e.g. RATS
It shines - STAR   LIVE
It's bad - EVIL

Once an anagram has been found, students can try to link the pairs in a sentence.

e.g. I pushed the **pram** up the **ramp**.
Take **care** if you want to win the **race**.
The **Nile** is a long **line** of water.

 **29** # Text Message
(Pairs)

Focus: Working out written messages

Level: Intermediate

Time: 10'+

Materials: Pencil, paper

Procedure:

Students play in pairs.
Students write coded messages to each other by leaving out the vowels in words and using single letters or numbers as part of the message.
The receiver decodes the message and writes it out in full, then replies in code.

e.g. Student A: h jhn. wht r u dng 2nght? d u wnt 2 cm rnd nd wtch th mtch?
[Hi John. What are you doing tonight? Do you want to come round and watch the match?]
Student B: sr, 8 k?
[Sure, Eight OK?]
Student A: grt. c u ltr.
[Great. See you later.]

What can you do with it?
30 (Groups)

Photocopiable Material: p. 143

Focus: Verb activation

Level: Intermediate

Time: 10'+

Materials: Cards

Procedure:

Divide the class into two groups and appoint a question master for the class.

Have students prepare noun cards – e.g. MEAT, CAR etc
The question master picks up a card, tells the word on t to group A. Group A has to think of an action you can do with it (a verb).
Group A thinks of something appropriate, then group B has to add another verb.
The game goes on until neither group can come up with a suitable verb.

e.g. **MEAT** – COOK, BOIL, ROAST, CHEW, FRY, BARBECUE, GRILL, SLICE, STIR-FRY, EAT

CAR – DRIVE, REVERSE, WASH, CRASH, PARK, RENT, REPAIR, WRECK, TOW, STOP

The winner is the last team to have added a verb which the question master accepts.

Sample Cards:

water	wall	hair	ball	pen	dog
book	banana	hat	flower	photo	CD

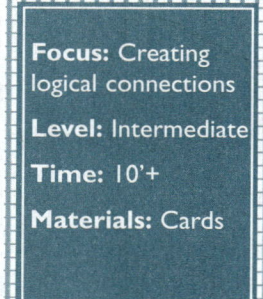

Only Connect
(Groups)

Photocopiable Material: p. 144

Focus: Creating logical connections

Level: Intermediate

Time: 10'+

Materials: Cards

Procedure:

Students play in groups of three.
Unrelated noun word cards are put in a pile face down on the table.
Student A picks up two cards, shows them to their group and tries to make a connection between them.

e.g. If the words picked up are BUTTERFLY and BATH, the connection might be:
- both make you feel good
- both come in different colours
- a butterfly looks more beautiful than what it came from- a caterpillar, and a bath makes you look more beautiful

If the other students accept the connection, student A keeps the cards.
If not, the cards are returned to the bottom of the pile and the next student plays.
All students have the same number of turns.

The winner is the student who collects the most cards.

Sample Cards:

| telephone | ball | card | door | book | water |

| piano | brush | apple | grass | fire | chain |

Variations:

- Make a comparison. e.g. A bath is heavier/ less colourful than a butterfly.
- Mime the words for your group to guess
- What can you do with it? Find 3 uses for an object apart from the usual. e.g. You could use a bath as a fish tank/ garden/ bed.
- Combine the words with a verb. e.g. Butterflies don't have baths.
- Use 3 or more cards and make up a story

Lost Letter
(Groups)

Photocopiable Material: p. 145

Focus: Guessing meaning, spelling

Level: Intermediate-Upper-intermediate

Time: 10'+

Materials: Cards

Procedure:

Students play in groups of three.

The game uses sentence cards in which one word has lost a letter, changing the meaning of the sentence.

Each card has one sentence and the changed word.

e.g.

> *He stepped on the **rake** hard to avoid a crash.*
>
> brake

Put sentence cards face down in the middle of the table.

Student A picks up a card and reads the sentence aloud to the rest of the group twice, at normal speed.

The other students decide which word has lost a letter and say what the changed word is.

If the group is unable to decide where the 'lost letter' goes, student A repeats the sentence at dictation speed for the group to write down.

If the group still cannot find the 'lost letter', student A says the missing letter, without telling the group which word it belongs to.

If nobody in the group can find the 'lost letter', then student A gives the correct answer and student B picks up the next card.

Students then create their own 'lost letter' sentence cards.

Sample Cards:

> *After the food, everything was washed away.*
>
> FLOOD

> *She liked to have a bat every day.*
>
> BATH

> *Remember to stain the pasta before you serve it.*
>
> STRAIN

> *A former runner won the Nobel pace prize today.*
>
> PEACE

> *She asked him round for a hat.*
>
> CHAT

> *The planes go round the sun.*
>
> PLANETS

> *She told him to dive home carefully.*
>
> DRIVE

> *We do not welcome idle treats, they said.*
>
> THREATS

> *They promised to enjoy the rest of their lies together.*
>
> LIVES

> *They protested against the lad being taken from them.*
>
> LAND

> *The manager said the defence has been sold all season*
>
> SOLID

> *She liked her fingers after the meal.*
>
> LICKED

Animal, Vegetable, Mineral
33
(Groups)

Photocopiable Material: p. 146

Focus: Word finding, asking questions

Level: Intermediate

Time: 10'+

Materials: Cards

Procedure:

Students play in groups of three.

Photocopy or prepare cards with various nouns on them. The cards should fit the categories: Animal, Vegetable or Mineral/Object.

Student A picks up a card and says what category it is in.

The other students in the group try and guess the word by asking yes/no questions.

The aim is to guess the word within 10 questions to win a point.

e.g. Student A: picks up [fridge]   *mineral/object.*

Student B: *Do you use it every day?*
Student A: *Yes.*
Student C: *Do you have one in the house?*
Student A: *Yes.*
Student B: *Is it smaller than you?*
Student A: *No.*   etc

Sample cards:

| watch | telephone | shark | ant | cup | hat |

| rose | butter | monkey | ring | ear | fork |

Variations:

- The word is stuck on a student's back with a pin and that student has to find it by asking questions.
- Students work in groups. A student from group A sits at the front of the class facing the others with his/her back to the board. A student from group B writes a word on the board and states the category. Student A, who cannot see the board, has to guess the word by asking yes/no questions of their group. A member of group B then takes A's place and student A writes a word for that student to find.

Near or Far
(Groups)

34

Photocopiable Material: p. 147

<table>
<tr><td>

Focus: Word relations

Level: Intermediate-Upper-intermediate

Time: 10'+

Materials: Cards, pencil, paper

</td><td>

Procedure:

Students play in groups of three.

Revise - opposites e.g. fast-slow, near-far, young-old,   etc
- synonyms e.g. happy-glad, quick-rapid, clever-bright,   etc
- word associations e.g. fast-food, near-sighted, young at heart,   etc

Photocopy or prepare starter cards. Give each group 10 starter word cards.
The first card is turned over and Student A has to find an opposite to this word.
Student B then has to find a synonym for either the word on the card or the one said by student A.
Student C then has to find a word associated with any of the preceding words.

</td></tr>
</table>

e.g.   Card: **fast**

Student A: *slow*
Student B: *quick*
Student C: *sand*

e.g   Card: **near**

Student A: *far*
Student B: *distant*
Student C: *horizon*

Sample cards:

high   **strong**   **wet**   **sweet**   **happy**   **short**   **hard**

One evening...
(Class)

35

<table>
<tr><td>

Focus: Quick thinking story making

Level: Advanced

Time: 15'+

Materials: Pencil, paper

</td><td>

Procedure:

Students make up a story - orally or written - one word at a time, going round the class.
The aim is to keep the story going as long as possible without ending the sentence.
Write the following words on the board: which, when, with, while, that, and, but, by, from, to, after, of, though.
Student A starts off a story and then each student has to continue the story by choosing a word which begins with the last letter of the previous word said.
If a student cannot think of a word, they can use one of the words on the board.
If one of these words is used, it is crossed off, and cannot be used again.
The next student has to begin their word as usual with the last letter of that word.
The game ends when a player cannot continue.
That player loses a point. The result can be quite funny and unexpected.

</td></tr>
</table>

e.g.   *One evening, George escaped daringly with hundreds of French hippopotami in nine enormous suitcases after realising that thirty yaks should damage English habits but too obvious sandwiches send dark koalas so obviously yelling 'good day'.*

2 Talking Together

Picture Board
(Groups)

Photocopiable material: pp. 148-149

Focus: Descriptive definitions

Level: Pre-intermediate - Intermediate

Time: 15'+

Materials: Board, counters, die/spinner, cards

Procedure:

Students play in groups of three.

Photocopy or prepare topic cards. Give each two groups a board, counters, word cards and a die/spinner and 20 topic cards. Groups move forward on the throw of the die/spin of the spinner.

When a group lands on a shaded square, they take a topic card from the face-down pile, turn it over and read the word out loud. Each member of the group has to say one different thing about the word on the card.

If they succeed, they keep the card and it is the other group's turn. If they can't think of anything else to say, the card is placed at the bottom of the pile and the other group rolls/spins.

If a group gets back to the Start square without having collected 5 cards, they continue around the board again.

The first team to collect 5 topic cards and return to the Start position wins.

e.g. Card: | rose |

Student A: *It's a flower.*
Student B: *It smells nice.*
Student C: *You can give it to a friend to show you love them.*

Alternative:

Group A picks up a card when they land on a shaded square, turns it face up and says one thing about it. Group B then says something else about the same topic. Groups continue to take turns until no one can say anything else relevant. The last group to say something relevant keeps the card and play continues.

Sample Cards:

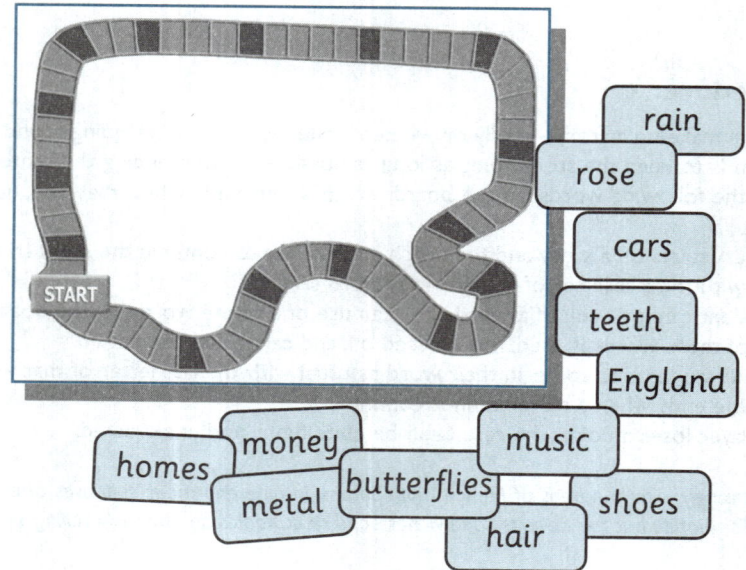

Who am I?
(Class)

Photocopiable material: p. 150

Photocopiable material: p. 150

☞ **Pointer:**

Choose names of characters that the students are likely to know

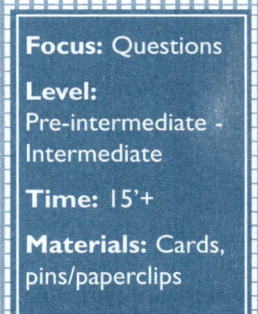

Focus: Questions

Level:
Pre-intermediate - Intermediate

Time: 15'+

Materials: Cards, pins/paperclips

Procedure:

Prepare cards, each with the name of a different famous person or fictitious character on it. Also, prepare three cards with a question mark on them for each student. Pin or clip a name card onto the back of each student so they cannot see it. Give each student three question mark cards. Students mingle with each other asking *Yes/No* questions to discover who they are.

e.g. *Am I male?*
Am I British?
Am I dead?
Am I a real person?

When a student thinks they know who they are, they can ask a question naming that person.
e.g. *Am I Madonna?*

If a student asks a question naming the person they think they are and gets a *no* answer, they must give one of their question cards to the other student. If a student loses all their question cards, they are out and can only answer questions from students still playing.

Sample Cards:

| Donald Duck | Laura Croft | Queen Elizabeth | William Shakespeare |

| Bill Gates | Mick Jagger | Elvis Presley | Alexander the Great |

Extension:

After the students find out who they are, they write a brief biography about that person/character.

Variation: What am I?

Instead of people, students must guess the names of objects. Pictures may be used instead of name cards.
When everybody knows what they are, select some objects to be interviewed.
In groups, students prepare information about their object and interview questions that they can ask another group.
Groups take it in turns to go up to the front of the class and be interviewed about their object.

Sample questions:

How old are you?
Who do you belong to?
How do they treat you?
Are you happy with your life?
What's the best thing that ever happened to you?

Sample Cards:

| mobile phone | passport | teddy bear | diary |

| bicycle | fridge | umbrella | key |

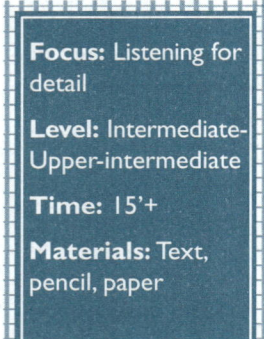

You cannot be serious!
(Groups)

Focus: Listening for detail

Level: Intermediate-Upper-intermediate

Time: 15'+

Materials: Text, pencil, paper

Procedure:

Students play in groups of three.

Prepare a brief version of your life story or an anecdote in which some of the facts are false. Read it to the class and ask the students to note down on paper how many false facts they think they heard by drawing Xs.   e.g. four false facts – XXXX

Repeat the story and the students take notes on what they think the false facts are.
In groups, students compare their notes and try to agree on what false facts they heard.

Give a copy of the text to each group and ask them to underline the false facts they have agreed on.
Groups swap texts. Read out the text again pausing at each false fact so that students may mark the papers.

If there were five false facts in the text, and a group correctly identified them, that group scores 5 points.
Groups then prepare their own texts, which they read to the class.

e.g.

> I was born at a very early age and said my first words at the age of one and a half. I was one of six children, who were all boys, and I am the oldest child in my family. My best subject at school was History, but I went to University to study Physics. I am now 26 years old and my greatest pleasure in life is to be in the classroom with you. My favourite animal (apart from humans) is the tiger, and in the future I would like to live in another country.

> Football began in England about 1000 years ago. Then they didn't have goals – you just had to get the ball from one village to another in any way you could. The first professional sides were formed more than 200 years ago and the most successful team ever is Brazil, which has won the world cup 6 times. Soccer is the most popular young peoples' sport in the USA. The women's USA team has been world champions. More people watch the world cup than the Olympic Games. There is a rule that says all goalkeepers must wear gloves. The oldest player in our national side is the goalkeeper.

Who, where, what, why?
(Pairs)

Photocopiable material: p. 151

Focus: Guessing context

Level: Intermediate

Time: 15'+

Materials: Cards, pencil, paper

Procedure:

Students play in pairs.
Write these questions on the board.

Who is the speaker?
Who are they speaking to?
Where are they?

What are they talking about?
Why are they having this conversation?
What could be the response?

Photocopy or prepare and give each pair a card which has part of a dialogue on it.
Pairs try to come up with a context for the expression on the card by answering the questions on the board. Then, they write a short dialogue including the phrase with at least three exchanges. The text on the card does not have to be the start of the dialogue. It can also be the middle or the ending.

e.g. **Card:**

> Mickey? What are you doing?

The pair decides that this is a mother to a child. The child is in another room and the mother can't see him. The mother may have heard a strange noise or perhaps is concerned because the child is too quiet.

e.g. Student A: Mickey? What are you doing?
Student B: Nothing mummy.
Student A: Well, come here where I can see you.

Each pair then takes it in turns to read out their card to the class. The other pairs decide what they think the situation is and what the exchanges might be. They write these down and then take turns to read them out. The pair with the original card listens to each exchange and awards a point to the pair who has written the most similar dialogue. Then they perform their exchange for the class.

The pair with the most points after all the exchanges have been read is the winner.

Sample Cards:

> What about Friday night then?

> See you outside at 8 then.

> That really wasn't necessary now, was it?

> You really don't get it, do you?

> I reckon that would be about right.

> I just went through the roof!

> Hurry up! It starts in ten minutes.

> It went like a dream.

> That's the third time this week. It really is too much!

> So. Who is she?

> Fine, thanks.

> Mickey? What are you doing?

Quiz Rummy
(Groups)

Photocopiable material: pp. 225-228

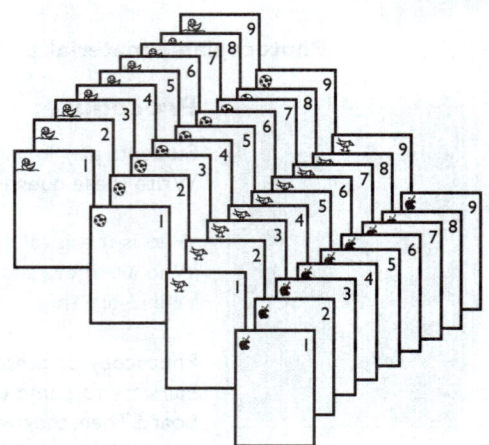

Focus: General knowledge

Level: Intermediate

Time: 20'+

Materials: Cards

Procedure:

Students play in groups of three.
Photocopy one set of 36 symbol cards for each group.

There are four symbol sets, each with nine cards numbered 1-9.
Choose subject areas to be represented by each symbol and write them on the board.

e.g.   = geography   = history
       = entertainment   = nature

Give each group one set of 36 cards and tell them what each symbol represents.
Students in the group share the cards and individually write a different general knowledge question and answer based on the subject the symbol on each card represents.

e.g.

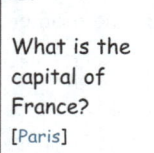

	I
What is the capital of France?	
[Paris]	

	I
What is the fastest animal?	
[Cheetah]	

	3
Where was Cleopatra from?	
[Egypt]	

	3
Who are Harry Potter's best friends?	
[Ron Weasley / Hermione Granger]	

Groups shuffle the cards and swap them with another group who does not look at what is written on them.
The cards are dealt out equally. The aim is to make sets of three or more cards of one symbol in numerical order (a run).
If student A has a run of three, they put these cards down, face up on the table.
Play proceeds clockwise around the table.

e.g.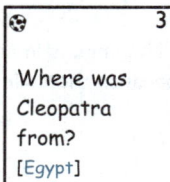

Students take it in turns to ask another student in the group if they have a card they need to complete a run.

e.g.   Student A: *Maria, do you have the 5 of entertainment?*
       Maria: *No, I don't.* (In this case, it is now student B's turn.)
       Maria: *Yes, I do.* (Maria now asks the question on the card to student A who must answer it correctly to receive that card.)
Student A puts down a run of three and it is now student B's turn.
If a player has a run of three, they must put it down.
The winner is the first student to get rid of all their cards or the one who has the most sets when nobody can go.

Variation:

Instead of general knowledge questions, choose four different language areas to practise.

e.g.   = verb tenses   = vocabulary
       = prepositions   = spelling

	8
If it is sunny, we .... (go) swimming.	
[will go]	

	3
Spell the word	
[communication]	

	4
Put the cake .... the oven.	
[in]	

	6
I have a ...... to WebNet Weekly.	
a. registration b. membership c. subscription	

What is it?
(Pairs)

Photocopiable material: p. 152

Focus: Asking questions, understanding references

Level: Intermediate

Time: 15'+

Materials: Cards

Procedure:

Students play in pairs.
Photocopy or prepare cards which have an object/event and a topic sentence on them.
Give each pair a set of ten cards, which they place face down on the desk.
Student A picks up a card and reads out the topic sentence without reading the object/event.
Student B has to find out what the object/event is – what the 'it' in each topic sentence refers to by asking Yes/No questions. Student A may help by saying such things as: *'You're getting warmer/colder'* and providing clues when needed.
Set a limit of ten questions for each word. If student B guesses the word, they win that card.
The winner is the student who has the most cards at the end of the game.

e.g. **Card:**

> **flood**
> It was awful. Everything indoors got wet so fast we couldn't stop it.

Student A: *It was awful. Everything indoors got wet so fast we couldn't stop it.*
Student B: *Is it the weather?*
Student A: *Warm!*
Student B: *Was it raining?*
Student A: *Yes it was. Not the word on my card though!*
Student B: *Was there a leak?*
Student A: *No, getting colder!*
Student B: (Can't think of anything to say, so student A gives a clue).
Student A: *Why did the animals go into the ark [big boat] 2 by 2?*
Student B: (Still can't think of anything.)
Student A: *Why would everything indoors get wet when it's raining and there's no leak?*
Student B: *There's a lot of water in the house from the rain?*
Student A: *Yes! Very warm!*
Student B: *Is it a flood?*
Student A: *Yes!*

Students then make up their own cards and pass them to other pairs to play.

Extension:

For higher levels: e.g. If student B guesses the word on the card they must write down a word that rhymes with it. Student A has three chances to guess what the word is. If student A guesses the word, they keep the card. If not student B keeps it.

Sample Cards:

> **flood**
> It was awful. Everything indoors got wet so fast we couldn't stop it.

> **exam**
> I couldn't believe how easy it was. I knew all the answers.

> **headache**
> I've already taken two, but it still won't go away.

> **printer**
> Well, it was working an hour ago. I suppose it's jammed again.

> **fire**
> They managed to put it out quickly and fortunately no one was hurt.

Get out alive!
(Groups)

Photocopiable material: pp. 153-154

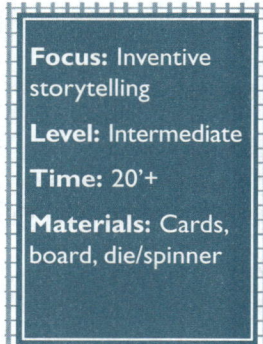

Focus: Inventive storytelling

Level: Intermediate

Time: 20'+

Materials: Cards, board, die/spinner

Procedure:

Students play in groups of three.

Tell students about the dangerous situation they must escape. e.g. stranded in the middle of a jungle

Give each group a copy of the board. Photocopy or have students prepare 20 cards with nouns that could be included in a jungle escape. The cards are shuffled and placed face down next to the board.

Students take it in turns to throw the die/spin the spinner to advance around the board.

If they land at the foot of a ladder, then they move up to the top of the ladder. If they land at the head of a snake, then they move down to the tail of the snake.

When a student lands on a smiley face ☺ or sad face ☹, they pick up a card.

If a student lands on a ☺, that student has to say how the object on the card helped them, even if it seems like a negative thing. If a student lands on a ☹, then they have to say how it caused a problem.

If a student throws/spins a 6, they get another turn.

Each student repeats the last part of the story (not necessarily using exactly the same words) and continues the story with each card picked up.

Card Pile

e.g.

Student A lands on a ☺ and picks up a card. helicopter

Student A: *I was lost in the jungle and very tired and hungry when I saw a helicopter overhead through the trees.*

Student B lands on a ☹ and picks up a card. water

Student B: *I was lost in the jungle and tired when I saw a helicopter through the trees but while I was looking up I slipped and fell into the water.*

Each student must add something which relates to what was previously said.

If a student cannot think of anything to say they miss their next turn.

The winner (who escapes from the jungle) is the one who gets to the end of the board first.

Sample Cards:

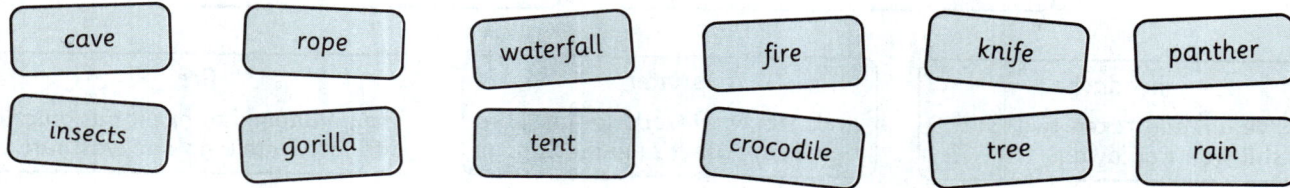

cave   rope   waterfall   fire   knife   panther

insects   gorilla   tent   crocodile   tree   rain

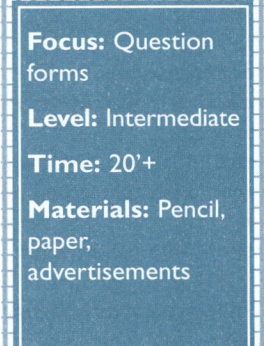

Define that product!
(Pairs)

Focus: Question forms

Level: Intermediate

Time: 20'+

Materials: Pencil, paper, advertisements

Procedure:

Students play in pairs.

Ask students to bring in as many magazine advertisements for different products as they can.

Share the advertisements among the students. Pairs look through the advertisements and decide on three different products.

Pairs then make up or choose from the advertising blurb, six different words or phrases which can describe the product without mentioning exactly what it is and write these on a piece of paper.

Two pairs play together.

Pair A starts by giving a clue to pair B who has to guess what the product is by asking *yes/no* questions.

If the answer is *yes*, pair B continues to ask *yes/no* questions. If the answer is *no*, then pair A gives the next clue.

If pair B finds the answer after one clue they score 6 points, after two clues 5 points, and so on.

The winner is the pair with the most points after each pair has presented its 3 products.

e.g.   Pair A's first product is a Jet Ski. They have written these 6 clues:

1. Mechanical   2. It moves   3. Summer fun   4. On the water   5. A motorbike   6. No wheels

Pair A: (clue 1) *Mechanical.*
Pair B: *Do we use it in the house?*
Pair A: *No.* (clue 2) *It moves.*
Pair B: *Do we use it for transport?*
Pair A: *Yes.*
Pair B: *Does it carry lots of people?*
Pair A: *No.* (clue 3) *Summer fun.*
Pair B: *Is it a jeep?*
Pair A: *No.* (clue 4) *On the water.*
Pair B: *Is it fast?*
Pair A: *Yes.*
Pair B: *Is it a boat?*
Pair A: *No.* (clue 5) *A motorbike.*
Pair B: *Is it a Jet Ski?*
Pair A: *Yes!*

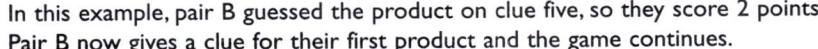

In this example, pair B guessed the product on clue five, so they score 2 points.

Pair B now gives a clue for their first product and the game continues.

Sample Products:

toothbrush, blow dryer, mobile phone, hair dye, laptop computer, soft drink, sports car, electric drill

Wrong number?
9 (Groups)

Photocopiable material: pp. 155-157

Focus: Telephone conversations

Level: Intermediate-Upper-intermediate

Time: 20'+

Materials: Cards, die/spinner, counters, board

Procedure:

Students play in groups of three.

Photocopy and give each group a copy of the board, caller and destination cards and counters.

Each student gets 5 caller and 10 destination cards. Caller cards have the place/person and purpose of the call written on them. Destination cards have just the place/person.

Students place their destination cards face up in front of them and their caller cards in a pile face down. Students place their counters on one of the start boxes and take it in turns to throw a die/spin a spinner. Students can move in any direction except diagonally. They can move up, down or across in one turn. The aim is to get to a telephone square. e.g. Student A throws/spins a 6: they can move 6 spaces in one direction or 2 upwards and 4 sideways, etc.

When they arrive on a telephone square they turn over their first caller card. They make a call starting with the words: *'Hello. Is that ...?'* The other students listen and if they have an appropriate destination card, they say *'Yes'*. If more than one student has that card, the first one to say *'Yes'* continues the conversation with the caller.

If no other student has an appropriate destination card, the caller puts that card in a 'fail' pile.

If the caller gets through to their destination, they have a conversation with the respondent to complete their task. When the task is completed, the caller takes the card from the respondent and places it with their caller card in a 'success' pile.

The first student to complete 5 calls is the winner.

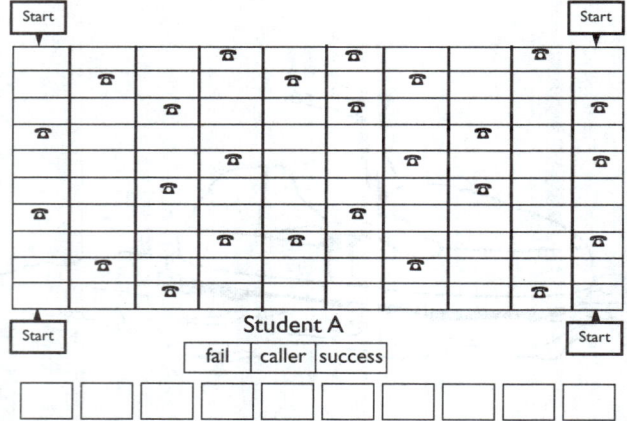

Student A

| fail | caller | success |

e.g. Card:

> Book a room
> Bay Hotel

Student A: *Hello. Is that the Bay Hotel?*
Student B: *Yes. How can I help you?*
Student A: *I'd like to book a room for next weekend.*
Student B: *Would that be a double or single room, sir?*
Student A: *Just a single, please.*
Student B: *Ok, sir. How many nights will you be staying?*
Student A: *Just the Saturday. Can you tell me how much that will be?*
Student B: *Forty-five Euros, sir, including breakfast. Could I have your name and phone number, please?* etc

Sample Caller Cards:

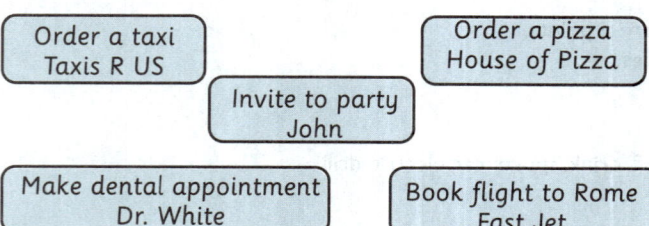

Order a taxi
Taxis R US

Order a pizza
House of Pizza

Invite to party
John

Make dental appointment
Dr. White

Book flight to Rome
Fast Jet

Sample Destination Cards:

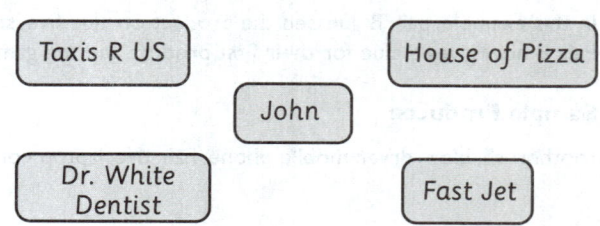

Taxis R US

House of Pizza

John

Dr. White
Dentist

Fast Jet

Alternative:

Students play in groups of six. Each student is assigned a number from 1-6 and has 5 caller and 5 destination cards.

Students take it in turns to throw the die /spin the spinner, pick up a caller card and call the person who has the number shown on the die/spinner. If the person called does not have the correct destination card, they say, *'Sorry wrong number.'* If that person has the correct destination card, a conversation takes place as above. When the conversation is completed, the caller takes the destination card and it is the next student's turn. The winner is the first to use all their caller cards.

What happens next?
(Pairs)

10

Photocopiable material: p. 158

☞ **Pointer:**

Giving students an activity such as scoring while listening, keeps them focused on the dialogue being performed.

Focus: Dialogue improvisation

Level: Intermediate-Upper-intermediate

Time: 20'+

Materials: Cards

Procedure:

Students play in pairs.
Give each student five cards, each with a different number – 1, 2, 3, 4, 5 – written on it.
Give pairs a situation card and tell them to decide who is going to take which role.
They can either improvise a dialogue or prepare and practise together first, then perform it in front of the class. Each dialogue must last at least 20 seconds.
For each role-play the rest of the class watches, and at the end of the performance, individually give the pair a score of 1-5 (5 being the top score) by holding up one of their 5 number cards.
Add up these numbers and write the score for each pair on the board.
When every pair has performed their dialogue, the winner is the pair with the best score.
Students then create their own situation cards.

e.g. Card:

> Your friend didn't meet you outside the cinema.
> (You want to find out why.)

Student A: *So why didn't you turn up? I missed the start of the film!*
Student B: *But I did! You weren't there!*
Student A: *Yes, I was – outside The Rialto at 9. That's what we agreed.*
Student B: *Yes, that's where I was – The Royalty.*
Student A: *The what?*
Student B: *The Royalty – 9 o'clock!*
Student A: *No, no. Not The Royalty – The Rialto!!!*

Sample Cards:

> You want to live in the city centre, but your roommate wants to live in the suburbs.
> (Find out why.)

> Your friend borrowed your car and scratched it badly.
> (You want to know how and what they are going to do about it.)

> Your flatmate refuses to do any housework, claiming you do it far better.
> (You want it to be shared equally.)

> Your boss refuses to give you a pay rise this year.
> (You want to know why.)

> Your best friend did not ring you on your birthday.
> (You want to know why.)

> Your best friend went to a party without you.
> (You want to know why.)

> You said your friend could stay in your flat for two nights, but s/he is still there after three weeks.
> (You want him/her to move out!)

> You are camping and find a strange person in your tent!
> (You want to know what they are doing there.)

> Your parents won't let you go on holiday with your friends.
> (You want to persuade them to let you.)

> Your friend didn't meet you outside the cinema.
> (You want to find out why.)

> Your parents don't want you to move away to study at university.
> (Find out why.)

> Your coach hasn't let you play many games this season.
> (Find out why.)

3 Bites [Initiate, respond, acknowledge]
11 (Pairs)

Photocopiable material: pp. 159-160

Focus: Short dialogues

Level: Intermediate

Time: 10'+

Materials: Cards

Procedure:

Students play in pairs.

Photocopy or prepare and give each pair a set of sentence cards and a set of response cards, which they place face down in front of them. The sentence cards have an opening dialogue sentence written on them and the response cards have a ⊕ or ⊖ sign on them.

Student A picks up a sentence card and at the same time, student B picks up a response card.

Student A reads out the sentence card. If student B has a ⊕ card, they have to make a positive response, expressing agreement or support. If student B has a ⊖ card, they have to make a negative response, expressing disagreement or criticism.

Student A then acknowledges this response in an appropriate way.

e.g. **Card:**

Student A: *I didn't think much of the meat.*
Student B: *But the salad was very good.*
Student A: *The salads are always tasty here.*

Student A: *I didn't think much of the meat.*
Student B: *Neither did I.*
Student A: *We won't come here again!*

It is now student B's turn to pick up a sentence card.

Students can also make their own opening sentence cards based on various situations or themes.

e.g.
Thematic – food, cinema, clothes, weather, etc.
Situational – at a restaurant, at the beach, at the bank, etc.
Controversial statements – e.g. You don't learn anything useful for real life at school.

All opening sentences should comprise natural sounding chunks of language.

Sample Cards:

Conversation Predictions
(Pairs)

Photocopiable material: p. 161

Focus: Short dialogue production

Level: Intermediate-Upper-intermediate

Time: 15'+

Materials: Cards, tape recorder, pencil, paper

Procedure:

Students play in pairs.

Photocopy or prepare situation cards and give the same situation card to each pair.

Pairs read the situation and write six phrases (of two - seven words) on a piece of paper that they would expect to hear in a dialogue in this situation.

Choose one pair to improvise a dialogue based on the phrases they have written, and perform it for the class. If possible, record the dialogue on tape.

The other students listen and tick off any phrases they hear that are the same as the ones they wrote down. If you have taped the dialogue, play it back so the students can check their answers.

The winner is the pair with the most correct predictions.

Play again with another situation card, choosing a different pair to perform their dialogue for the class.

e.g. **Card:**

> You want your parents to buy you a motorbike for your 17th birthday.

Why not	They're dangerous
But ... has got one	You know what I'd like
You're too young	Absolutely not!

e.g. Student A: *What would you like for your birthday, Steven?*
Student B: *You know what I'd like.*
Student A: *What would that be?*
Student B: *I'd like a motorbike for my birthday.*
Student A: *Absolutely not!*
Student B: *Why not?*
Student A: *You're too young.*
Student B: *I'm going to be 17 next month.*
Student A: *They're dangerous.*
Student B: *But Jason has got one.*

Sample Cards:

> You visit the dentist after a long time.

> Your flatmate has not paid her share of the rent for 6 months.

> You have just returned from an awful holiday and your friend asks you about it.

> You didn't go to school yesterday and the teacher wants to know why.

> You have a car accident and report it to the police.

> A policeman stops you when you are riding your motorbike.

> You have a job interview.

> A UFO lands in front of your house and an alien gets out.

> Your best friend doesn't want to see you any more.

How high can you go?
(Groups)

13

Photocopiable material: p. 162

Focus: Giving reasons, justifying

Level: Intermediate-Upper-intermediate

Time: 15'+

Materials: Cards, board, die/spinner

Procedure:

Students play in groups of four to six.

Give each group a board and six word cards based on the same theme. e.g. Football – different jobs connected to the game of football – chairman, manager, captain, substitute, groundsman, boot cleaner. The word cards are placed face down next to the board. Each student picks a card without saying or showing the word to the other students. Students take it in turns to give clues to the rest of the group, who try to guess who they are.

e.g.   Student A: *I make sure the grass is cut. Who am I?*
Student B: *The groundsman.*
Student A: *Correct!*

When all the words have been guessed, the students throw a die/spin a spinner to determine what position they will have on the board. If a student rolls/spins a number and the position has already been filled, they must try again until they find a free space on the grid. e.g. Student D has the Captain card and rolls/spins a 6. Student D will write Captain in postion 6 in the first grid on the board.

When all the students know what position they are, they place their word cards in the corresponding space on the second grid on the board.

Students now take it in turns, starting from the student in position 6, to give reasons/explain why their particular job deserves a better place of importance than they have. (1 - most important, 6 - least important)

For each reason a student gives, their card moves up one position. Each student is allowed only one turn to give their reasons.

Original Position		Final Position	
1	Groundsman	1	
2	Manager	2	
3	Boot cleaner	3	
4	Chairman	4	
5	Substitute	5	
6	Captain	6	CAPTAIN

e.g.   Student D is in position 6. This student feels that being Captain of the football team is a very important position and thinks of three reasons why.

Student D: *I organise the team during the game. I decide who takes penalties. The manager relies on me more than the other players.*

Student D now moves up 3 places to postion 3, and the boot cleaner moves to position 6.

No 5, the substitute gives one reason, so they exchange places with no 4, the chairman.

No 4, the chairman gives four reasons, so they exchange places with no 1, the groundsman

Original Position		Final Position	
1	Groundsman	1	MANAGER
2	Manager	2	CHAIRMAN
3	Boot cleaner	3	GROUNDSMAN
4	Chairman	4	BOOT CLEANER
5	Substitute	5	CAPTAIN
6	Captain	6	SUBSTITUTE

The boot cleaner (now in position 6) gives two reasons, so they exchange places with the substitute.

No 2, the manager gives one reason, so they exchange places with the chairman (who is now in position 1).

The groundsman (now in position 5) gives two reasons, so they exchange places with the captain (now in postion 3).

The winner is the student whose final place is position 1.

Other possible themes:

Pets	Famous People	Art Forms	Countries	Foods
Jobs	Dwellings	Types of Holiday	Media	Music

Do you come here often?
(Pairs)

14

Photocopiable material: pp. 225-228

Focus: Dialogue creation

Level: Intermediate

Time: 15'+

Materials: Cards

Procedure:

Students play in pairs.

Prepare or photocopy sets of 40 symbol cards. Each set has 4 different symbols and each symbol pattern has ten cards each, numbered 1 to 10.

e.g.

 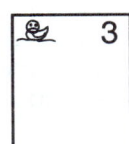  

Shuffle each set of the 40 symbol cards and divide it between two pairs, giving 20 cards to each pair. Each student takes 10 cards. The students place their cards face down in a pile in front of them.

Student A turns over their first card, places it in the middle of the table and starts a conversation. Each phrase the students say must have the same number of words as the number on the card.

e.g. 7 🦅 = 7 words

Contractions may count as either one or two words.

If a student puts down a card which has the same number or symbol as the previous one, they can win all the cards in the pile by using that number of words to finish the conversation. The cards they win are placed under their pile of face down cards.

e.g. Student A puts down 2 🦆: *Hi there.*
Student B puts down 7 🍎: *Hi, I haven't seen you for ages.*
Student A puts down 8 🦅: *Well, I've been away on holiday in Spain.*
Student B puts down 4 ⚽: *Nice tan you've got.*
Student A puts down 6 ⚽: *Yes, the weather was great. Bye.*

Student A put down the 6 ⚽ card, which has the same symbol as the previous card down. Student A used 6 words to finish the conversation and therefore picks up all the cards and puts them at the bottom of their pile. Student B starts a new conversation by putting down a new card.

The game continues until one of the students has no cards left. The winner is the one with all the cards.

For lower levels, use only the cards numbered 1-5.

Alternatives:

1) The same as above, but students write down their sentences as well as saying them orally.

2) Instead of using cards, students use a die/spinner so the maximum number of words each turn is six. When a student throws/spins the same number as in the previous turn, they finish the conversation with that many words and win a point. The winner is the first to get 5 points.

That's why I need it
15 (Groups)

Photocopiable material: pp. 163-164, 232

Focus: Persuading, making connections

Level: Intermediate

Time: 15'+

Materials: Cards

Procedure:

Students play in groups of three.

Give each group a set of job cards and a set of object cards, which they place face down in two piles on the table.

Students take it in turns to pick up a card from each pile and try to justify to the rest of the group why the object would be useful to the job.

If they give a good reason which is accepted by the other students, they keep both cards. If the reason is not accepted, then the student to the right gets a chance to give an answer. If no one in the group can find a reasonable connection between the object and the job, then both cards are placed at the bottom of the respective piles.

The game continues until there are no cards left or students cannot make a connection between the remaining cards. In this case, the piles are shuffled and play continues.

The winner is the student with the most cards at the end of the game.

e.g. **Cards:**   baker   chalk

Student A: *The baker can use the chalk to write the prices of their breads on a board outside the shop.*

Sample job cards:

postman   gardener   bus driver   detective   electrician   teacher

Sample object cards:

flower   camera   hammer   paint   earring   drum

Alternative:

Give each group a board with different objects on it and a spinner/die.

Give each student a job card and a counter. Students take it in turn to throw or spin to move their counter. When they land on an object space, they have to say why that object would be useful in their job. If they make an acceptable connection they move the number of spaces they last rolled /spun. If not, they go back that number of spaces.

The winner is the first to get to the end of the board.

FINISH		rope	camera	bucket	←
→	torch		needle		
				drum	
chalk		paint		fish	←
→	music CD		whistle		gloves
hammer		earring	violin		←
START →		dog	ball	flower	paper clip

Survivor
(Pairs)

Focus: Presenting a case

Level: Intermediate-Upper-intermediate

Time: 15'+

Materials: Roles

Procedure:

Students play in pairs.

Assign each pair a role – a job or a famous person in a different field. Write the roles on the board. Allow pairs three minutes to prepare a case on why their job or person is more important/valuable than the others. Pairs present their case in front of the class.

After all the pairs have given their presentation, the other pairs can challenge their claims. The class then votes on who should survive. Pairs are not allowed to vote for themselves.

e.g. Pair A: 'Teacher' - *We feel that being a teacher is the most important job because without teachers there would be no other jobs. Nobody would learn anything. Also, teachers influence a lot of young people in positive ways. Sometimes children see teachers more than their parents, so they are very important in helping and guiding young people, not just teaching.*

Sample Roles:

teacher
famous scientist
rock star
lawyer
famous athlete
doctor
car manufacturer
sales person

Alternative:

1) Instead of people, students are assigned an object – television, mobile phone, fridge, computer etc, and must justify why theirs is the most important.

2) Pair A competes against pair B, pair C against pair D, etc. The class votes to eliminate pairs one by one until there is just one pair left, who is the winner.

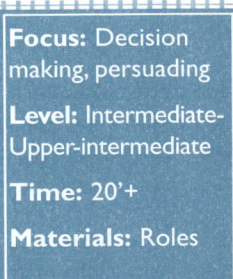

Watch this space
(Groups)

Focus: Decision making, persuading

Level: Intermediate-Upper-intermediate

Time: 20'+

Materials: Roles

Procedure:

Students play in groups of three.

Provide or get students to draw a map of the local area with all the shops, businesses and amenities that already exist, as well as the building/area to be improved.

Tell the class that a building/area in your town is due for redevelopment. Give each group a list of roles. Each student picks a role from the list or chooses their own. The groups have a meeting to decide what to do with the building/area from the point of view of the role they have chosen. Allow five minutes for the groups to come up with their arguments and make a final decision. Groups pick one person to present their case to the class. After each group is heard, the class votes on who they feel presented the best argument.

Chemist	Hospital	Gym
	Richmond Street	
Bank	Town Square	Supermarket
High Street	Centre Street	Hudson Street
Library	School	Restaurant

Sample Roles:

mayor	mother with 3 children
ecologist	fast food owner
athlete	homeless person
17 year old	property developer
teacher	museum curator
pensioner	shop owner
secretary	supermarket manager

e.g. The town square is going to be developed.
  17 year old: *I think young people need a place to meet ... like a cafe.*
  Pensioner: *They should make it a garden with lots of trees - a quiet place to visit.*

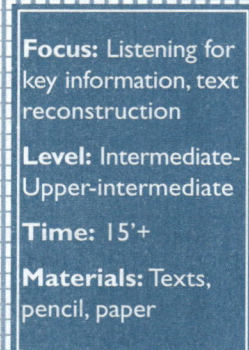

How I got my scar
(Pairs)

Focus: Listening for key information, text reconstruction

Level: Intermediate-Upper-intermediate

Time: 15'+

Materials: Texts, pencil, paper

Procedure:

Students play in pairs.

Write a short story or anecdote which has a personal theme.

Read the text twice, at normal speed, and have the students just listen.

Read the text a third time and ask students to write down up to ten key words that they hear.

In pairs, students compare information, tick off words they have in common, and agree on the order of the words/events they have noted.

Students reconstruct and write the story from their notes.

Sample Text:

It was sometime last June, and I was cycling home from work. It was about 9 pm, and I was taking my usual route home. I don't remember exactly what happened, but they tell me a car hit me from behind. Anyway, I woke up in hospital and the doctor said that I had a badly broken arm. He said that they could either put it in plaster for a few months, to see if the bone healed properly, or they could operate and put a metal pin in there to hold the bone together. I told them to operate and that's why I have this big long scar from my shoulder to almost my elbow.

Sample Key Words:

Student A:	Student B:
June – cycling – 9 pm – car – hospital – arm – plaster – operate – scar – elbow	last June – work – about – remember – behind – hospital – broken – plaster – pin – scar

Sample reconstructed text from students A and B:

Sometime last June I was coming home from work by bicycle. It was about 9 o'clock in the evening. I don't remember how it happened but a car behind me hit me. I woke up in hospital with a broken arm. The doctor said they could put it in plaster for several months or they could operate and put a pin there to join the bones together. I said operate, which is why I have a big scar from my shoulder to my elbow.

Pairs swap their papers. Read the original text again slowly or show it on an overhead projector and have students mark the papers in front of them. Give points for words/information found in the original in the right place and deduct points for words/information not in the original.

The pair with the most points is the winner.

Other possible topics:

My best holiday
My most embarrassing moment
My proudest moment
My most frightening experience
The funniest thing that happened at school

Students can write their own texts and take it in turns to read their anecdote for the rest of the class to reconstruct.

What have you got there?
(Groups)

Photocopiable material: p. 165

Focus: Questions and guessing

Level: Intermediate

Time: 15'+

Materials: Board, counters, cards

Procedure:

Students play in groups of four.

Give each group a copy of the board, 4 counters and 8 blank cards - 2 per student.

Each student writes the name of a different item/product on each card. e.g. fridge, computer, bottle

The cards are shuffled and passed face down to another group.

Student A picks up a card, reads it and places it face down in the centre space of the board without letting the others see it.

The other students place their counters in their own start box on the board. Students take it in turns to ask student A *'yes/no'* questions to find out what item/product is written on the card.

e.g. *'Can you eat it?' 'Is it made of metal?' 'Is it bigger than me?'*   etc.

If a student receives a *'yes'* answer, they move forward one space. If a student receives a *'no'* answer, they stay where they are.

When a student reaches the 5th square, they can ask a direct question to identify the item/product.   e.g. *'Is it a fridge?'*

If the student has not guessed correctly, they stay where they are and the game continues.

If they have guessed correctly, they win the card in the centre.

It is now student B's turn to pick up a card and answer questions from the other students.

The winner is the student with the most cards after all the students in the group have had two turns answering questions.

Sample Board:

What's hot?
20 (Pairs)

Photocopiable material: p. 166

Focus: Comparing and justifying

Level: Upper-intermediate

Time: 15'+

Materials: Cards, pencil, paper

Procedure:

Students play in pairs. Two pairs play against each other.
Photocopy or make cards which have two similar products/ideas on them.
Give each two pairs a card.
Pair A must think of reasons why the **A** product/idea on the card is better or more 'in' than the **B** product/idea. Pair B must do the same for their product/idea.

Allow pairs 2 minutes to discuss and note down points in favour of their product/idea and against the other. The A and B pairs share their ideas and discuss why they think their product/idea is best.
Sets of pairs present their case in front of the class for 1 minute.
The class then votes on who they think presented the best case for their product/idea.

e.g.   **Card:**

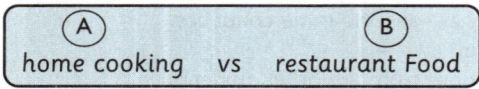

Pair A: *We think home cooking is better than restaurant food because it's healthier.*
Pair B: *We think restaurant food is better because you can get anything you like, including healthy options.*
Pair A: *Well, you can make anything you like at home and in anyway you like it. Restaurant food is usually made and served the way the chef makes it.*
Pair B: *Restaurant food is also better because you don't have to go to the fuss of making your meal or cleaning up afterwards!* **etc.**

Sample Cards:

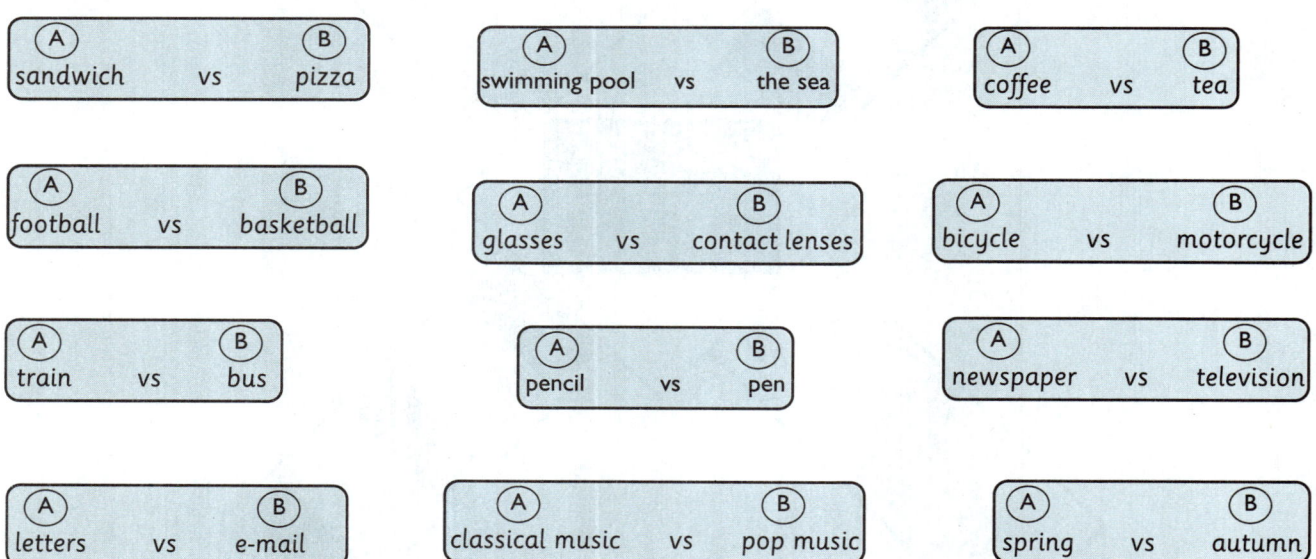

That says a lot about you
21 (Groups)

Photocopiable material: pp. 167 & 177

Focus: Giving opinions, describing

Level: Intermediate

Time: 15'

Materials: Board, cards, counters, die/spinner

Procedure:

Students play in groups of four.

Give each group a ludo board, 4 counters, a die/spinner and a set of category cards. The cards are placed face down in a pile on the table. Students can make their own category cards.

Each student places a counter in their own start box. Students take it in turns to roll/spin to get around the board. Students move around the squares on the outside of the board until they come back to their own starting area, where they move up the blue squares to the home position.

When a student lands on a space with a **?**, they pick up a category card and think of some item/product in that category which they like and talk about it. Students must include three reasons why they like the item/product and are not allowed to use the words GOOD or NICE.

If a student can give three reasons, they keep that card. If not, the card goes to the bottom of the card pile. If a student lands on a space already occupied by another student, they knock that student back to the start position.

The winner is the person who has the most cards when they reach the HOME position.

e.g. Student A: *I really like sarongs because you can use them as a dress in the summer. They are usually colourful and keep you cool.*

Sample Board:

Sample Cards:

clothes

food

books

films

flowers

festivals

cars

countries

colours

animals

sports

cities

Bon Voyage!
(Groups)

Photocopiable material: pp. 168-169

Photocopiable material: pp. 168-169

☞ **Pointer:**

This game can be adapted and used with a map of any area you are familiar with. e.g. cities/islands in your country, local landmarks, etc.

Focus: Improvised speaking

Level: Upper-intermediate – Advanced

Time: 25'+

Materials: Board, die/spinner, counters, cards

Procedure:

Students play in groups of three.

Enlarge the map on a photocopier and give each group a copy of the map board, counters, die/spinner and cards.

The cards are placed face down on the table.

Each student takes five cards and turns them over. These are the five islands they must *visit* in order to win the game. The rest of the cards remain face down in a pile.

Each student places their counter on one of the two start positions and plans the best route to get to all their islands.

Students take it in turns to roll/spin and move around the islands on the board. Students try to be the first to visit all their islands and return to their original start position.

When a student arrives on one of the islands written on one of their cards, they have 30 seconds to talk about the name of that island. If they can speak for 30 seconds, they keep the card. If not, they put the card at the bottom of the card pile and pick up a new island card to add to the ones they need to visit. The winner is the first student to visit all five of their islands and return to their original start position.

Student A: Has ┌─ ROSE ISLAND ─┐ and lands on it.   *A rose is a flower which you can find in many different colours and types. There are climbing roses and rose bushes. Although they are very beautiful, roses have sharp thorns .... etc.*

Sample Cards:

HEART ISLAND   CAVE ISLAND   RABBIT ISLAND   STAR ISLAND   BUTTERFLY ISLAND   KEY ISLAND

SHOE ISLAND   VOLCANO ISLAND   BIRD ISLAND   DIAMOND ISLAND   BELL ISLAND   DOLPHIN ISLAND

23 One Word Stories
(Groups)

Focus: Story building

Level: Upper-intermediate - Advanced

Time: 15'+

Materials: Toothpicks

Procedure:

Students play in groups of three.

Students tell a story, one word at a time. Every second word must be one syllable.

Each student starts with 10 toothpicks and wins or loses them depending on their progress in the game.

Students lose a toothpick if :
- they cannot continue
- they add a word which does not make sense
- they add a word of the wrong syllable length

Students gain a toothpick if they add a word which finishes a sentence and the next student cannot continue.

The winner is the student who has the most toothpicks at the end of a time limit.

e.g.
Student A: *One*
Student B: *morning*
Student C: *I*
Student A: *wandered*
Student B: *down*
Student C: *market*
Student A: *street*
Student B: (cannot think of a word of two syllables or more – student B loses a toothpick and student A gains a toothpick as they have finished the sentence. Student C continues by starting a new sentence.)
Student C: *Suddenly*
Student A: *in*
Student B: *Mario's*
Student C: *I*
Student A: *noticed*
Student B: *a*
Studnet C: *horrible*
Student A: *fat*
Student B: *cockroach*
Student C: *eat*   etc.

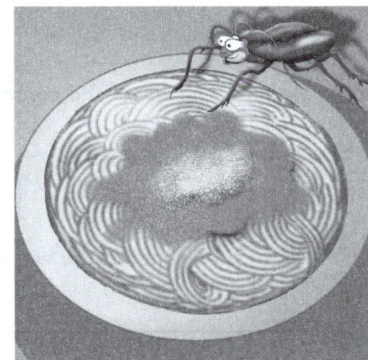

The story can be strange and this adds to the fun. Students have to think on their feet about vocabulary, sentence structure, collocation and logic.

3 Vocabulary

Conundrum
(Pairs)

Photocopiable material: pp. 229-231

Focus: Spelling, word building

Level: Elementary - Intermediate

Time: 10'+

Materials: Letter tiles, paper, pencil

Procedure:

Students play in pairs. Two pairs play against each other.
Give each two pairs 25 letter tiles: 10 vowel tiles and 15 consonant tiles.

The tiles are placed face down in two separate piles - vowels and consonants.
Pair A begins by calling out either *'vowel'* or *'consonant'*. Pair B picks up a tile from that pile and turns it over. Pair A then calls out for another *'vowel'* or *'consonant'* and pair B turns that tile over.
Pair A continues to call out *'vowel'* or *'consonant'* until there are seven tiles face up on the table.

Pairs now have one minute to make the longest word they can from the chosen letters.
Letters can only be used once. Each letter is worth one point. The pair with the longest word wins that round.

e.g.　**Letter Tiles:**　O　P　E　N　S　M　A

Pair A:　M　A　P　S

Pair B:　M　O　A　N　S

Pair B has the longest word and scores 5 points. The vowel and consonant tiles are shuffled and the pairs start a new round with pair B calling for a *'vowel'* or *'consonant'*.
The pair with the most points after 5 rounds wins the game.

Variation:

Use scrabble letters with their letter score, so the winner at the end is not just the pair with the longest word in each round, but also the highest letter scores.

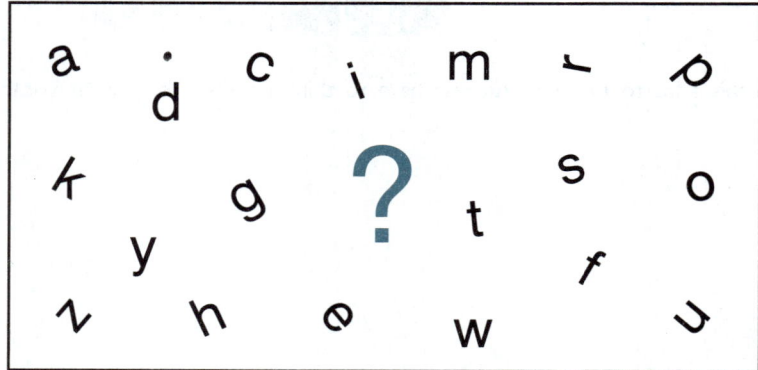

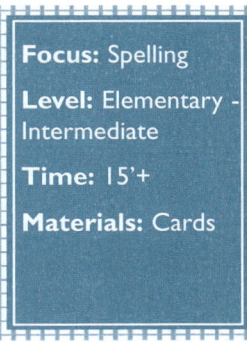

Scissors, Paper, Stone
(Groups)

Focus: Spelling

Level: Elementary - Intermediate

Time: 15'+

Materials: Cards

Procedure:

Students play in groups of three.

Prepare and give each group a set of 30 different word cards. Choose words students may have difficulty spelling. The cards are shuffled and placed face down in the centre of the table.

Students take it in turns to play Scissors, Paper, Stone with the person on their right. The loser of each round picks up a word card and reads it to the winner who must spell that word.

If the winner spells the word correctly, they keep the card. If not, the card is returned to the bottom of the pile. Student B now plays with student C and the game continues. The winner is the student who has the most word cards at the end of ten rounds.

> ### Scissors, Paper, Stone
>
> In the traditional children's game, players count to three together and on the count of three make one of the above three shapes with their hand
>
> Scissors beats paper [they can cut it], paper beats a stone [it can wrap it], and a stone beats scissors [it can blunt them].

Variation:

To practise different lexical areas.

1   Prepare three sets of 10 cards.
    Scissor word cards: nouns, Paper word cards: verbs, Stone word cards: adjectives. Students play the game as above. The winner has to spell the word correctly and then put it in a complete sentence.

2   Prepare three sets of 10 cards.
    Scissor word cards: spell the word, Paper word cards: give a definition, Stone word cards: say a word which rhymes with it.

    In both variations, the winner is the one who has the most cards at the end of ten rounds.

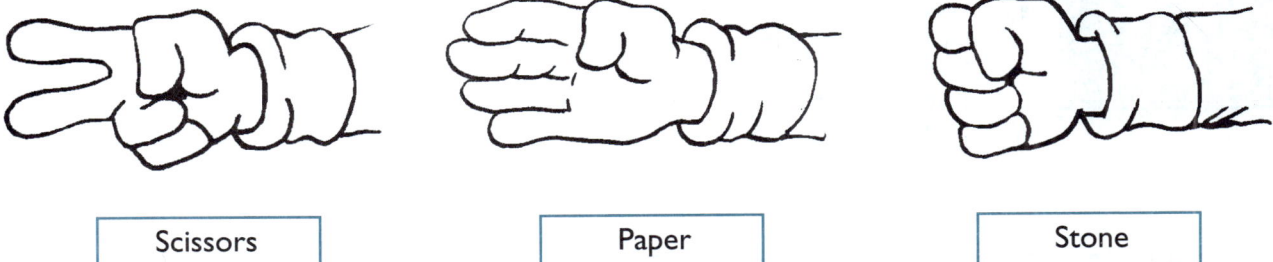

| Scissors | Paper | Stone |

Mobile Phone Codes
3 (Pairs)

Focus: Spelling, word reinforcement
Level: Elementary - Intermediate
Time: 15'+
Materials: Paper, pencil

Procedure:

Students play in pairs.

Draw a large picture of a mobile phone keypad on the board. Student A thinks of a word and writes it down without letting student B see it. Student A looks at the keypad and says the numbers that correspond to the letters of his secret word. Student B writes down the letters that each number corresponds to and tries to find student A's word.

e.g   Student A: *4, 6, 8, 7, 3* (house)
            Student B: 4 = G H I
                       6 = M N O
                       8 = T U V
                       7 = P Q R S
                       3 = D E F

If student B finds the word they get a point. If more than one word is possible, student B has to decide which word is **student A's secret word**. It is now student B's turn to make up a secret word.
The winner is the first one to get 10 points or the student with the most points after an agreed time/word limit.

Reverse Spelling
4 (Pairs)

> ☞ **Pointers:**
> * Use shorter words for lower levels.
> * Make a list of words your students often misspell and write them on cards for students to use.

Focus: Spelling
Level: Pre-intermediate - Intermediate
Time: 10' +
Materials: Pencil, paper

Procedure:

Students play in pairs.

Student A thinks of a word and writes it down without letting student B see it. Student A tells student B how many letters the word has and then starts spelling the word slowly in reverse order.

Student B writes down the letters being dictated. After each letter, student B has a chance to guess what they think the word is. If student B is correct, they get one point for each letter left in the word (letters that student A did not read out). If student B makes a wrong guess at any stage, they lose a point.

e.g.   Student A: *S*
          Student B: (not ready to guess)
          Student A: *I*
          Student B: (not ready to guess)
          Student A: *N*
          Student B: (not ready to guess)
          Student A: *N*
          Student B: *TENNIS!*

Student B guessed the word with 2 letters left and therefore gets 2 points.
Each student has 5 turns at spelling and 5 turns at guessing. The winner is the student with the most points at the end of the game.

Variation:

Student A dictates all the letters of the word without pause, again in reverse order.
Student B writes down as many letters as they can remember and then tries to guess the word.
Students win a point for each word they guess correctly.

Blockbuster

(Pairs)

Photocopiable material: pp. 167, 170, 181

Focus: Any lexical area

Level: Pre-intermediate-Intermediate

Time: 15'+

Materials: Board, coloured pencils, topic cards

Procedure:

Students play in pairs.

Prepare or photocopy and give each pair a board, a set of topic cards and coloured pencils. The board is a 5 x 5 grid of hexagons which have a different letter written in them. The topic cards can be any topic you wish to practise. Student A chooses a coloured pencil (e.g. grey) and student B chooses a different coloured one (e.g. blue).

Student A turns over a topic card and chooses a letter hexagon on the grid. Student A must say a word, beginning with this letter, related to the chosen topic. If both the students agree that the word is appropriate, then student A colours that hexagon grey. Student B now chooses a different letter hexagon and says a word beginning with that letter. If neither student can think of a word, they turn over a new topic card and continue the game.

Students have to get across the grid, either top to bottom or side to side by creating a linked bridge of their own colour. At all times students try to block their opponent's progress. The winner is the first one to get across the grid.

e.g. Topic Card: Animals

Student A: Letter C: *Cat*
Student B: Letter T: *Tiger*
Student A: Letter F: *Fox*
Student B: Letter E: *Elephant*
Student A: Letter H: *Horse*
Student B: Letter D: *Dog* (Blocks student A's progress)
Student A: Letter O: *Ostrich*   etc.

Sample topics:

animals
clothes
food
places
sports

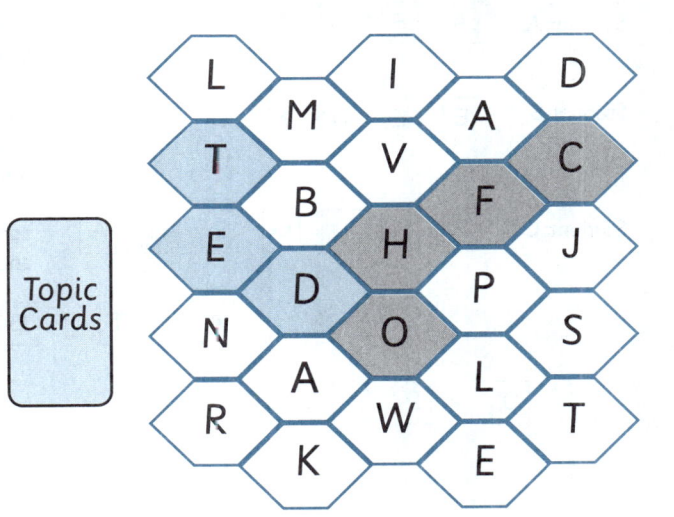

Variation:

Write prepositions in each hexagon. Students have to come up with a phrasal verb used in a meaningful sentence to win that hexagon.

e.g. Student A: (hexagon says OUT): *I can't work out the answer to this question.*

Correct, meaningful use of the phrasal verb wins that hexagon.

Scrabble
(Groups)

Photocopiable material: pp. 229-231

Focus: Spelling, word building

Level: Pre-intermediate-Intermediate

Time: 15'+

Materials: Letter tiles

Procedure:

Students play in groups of three.
Photocopy or prepare a set of letter tiles for each group. Put each set of tiles in a bag or envelope.

Each student takes 7 letters from the bag/envelope.
Students take it in turns to look at their letters and make words which they put on the table.

Student A uses their letter tiles to make a word and places it in the centre of the table. Student A then takes the same number of letter tiles they used to make their word from the bag/envelope, so that they have 7 letter tiles again.
Student B must now make a new word using one of the letters in the word student A has put down. Students can add a letter or letters to the beginning or end of words already down on the table to create a new one. The letter added can also form part of a new word. Students make words which run either across or down. All letters score one point.

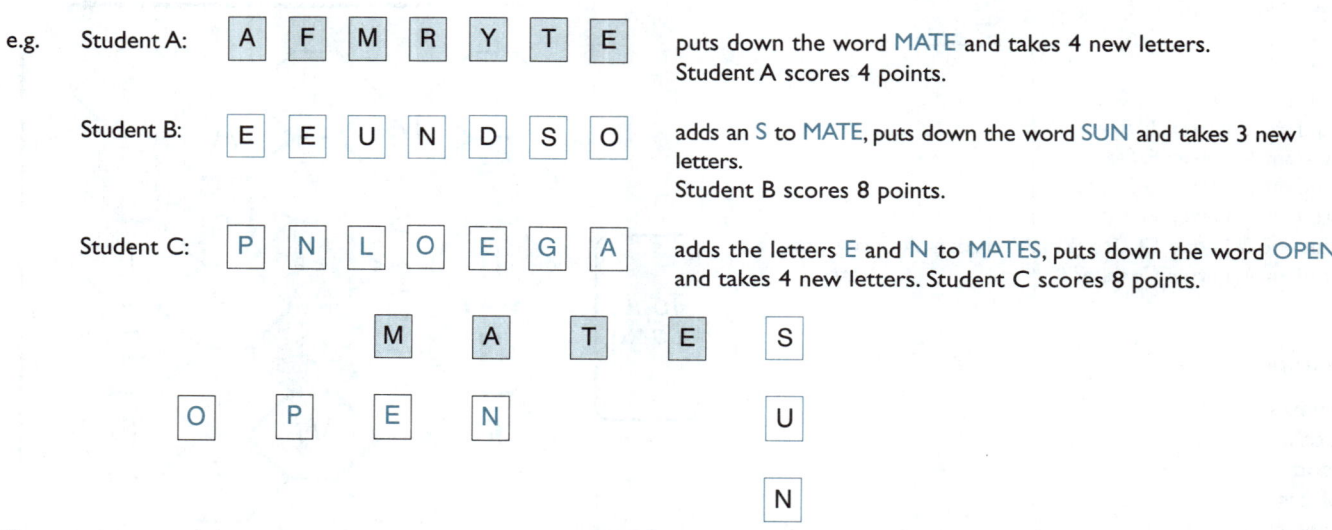

e.g.   Student A: A F M R Y T E   puts down the word MATE and takes 4 new letters.
Student A scores 4 points.

Student B: E E U N D S O   adds an S to MATE, puts down the word SUN and takes 3 new letters.
Student B scores 8 points.

Student C: P N L O E G A   adds the letters E and N to MATES, puts down the word OPEN and takes 4 new letters. Student C scores 8 points.

```
      M   A   T   E   S
  O   P   E   N       U
                      N
```

Play continues until there are no letter tiles left in the bag/envelope, one student has put down all their letters or nobody can put letters anywhere to make a word. The winner is the student with the most points.

Variation:

Students take 10 letter tiles and have to use all of them to make words. Students can put down more than one word each turn but do not replace their letter tiles. On their next turn they can throw back as many of their remaining letters as they wish into the bag/envelope and replace them with different ones. If a student exchanges letters on their turn, they must wait until their next turn to form words.
The winner of each round is the first to get rid of all 10 letter tiles.

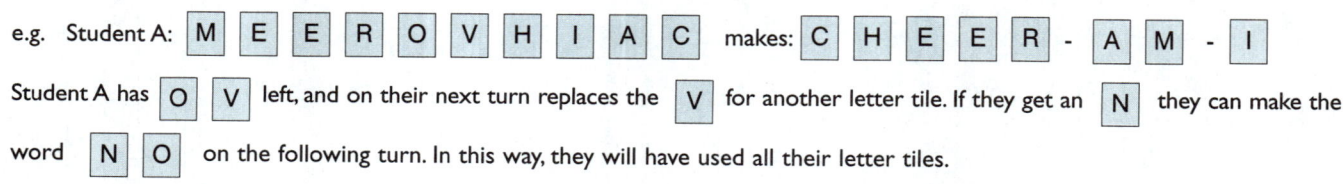

e.g.   Student A: M E E R O V H I A C   makes: C H E E R - A M - I

Student A has O V left, and on their next turn replaces the V for another letter tile. If they get an N they can make the word N O on the following turn. In this way, they will have used all their letter tiles.

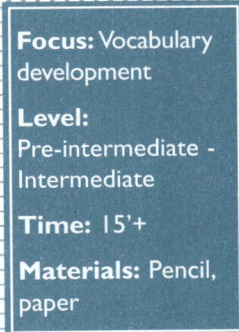

Get Packing
(Groups)

Focus: Vocabulary development

Level: Pre-intermediate - Intermediate

Time: 15'+

Materials: Pencil, paper

Procedure:

Students play in groups of three.

In groups, students brainstorm and come up with 3 lists of 10 items each: Clothing, Food, and Other/Miscellaneous. These items represent things they would like to have with them if they were ever stranded on a desert island. The more unusual the items the better.

Groups take it in turns to read out loud the items on their lists. As the items are read, the other groups listen and cross off any items they hear that they also have on their lists.

e.g.

Group A

Clothing	Food	Other
~~trousers~~	grapes	~~compass~~
~~t-shirt~~	coffee	~~tent~~
jeans	meat	blanket
tie	~~bread~~	lighter
~~shirt~~	tomatoes	rope
belt	olives	mobile phone
trainers	rice	~~knife~~
~~socks~~	lettuce	mirror
~~boots~~	cheese	map
~~jacket~~	peanuts	~~radio~~

TOTAL POINTS: 19

Group B

Clothing	Food	Other
shorts	chocolate	torch
~~shirt~~	apples	~~tent~~
sandals	~~milk~~	sleeping bag
~~jacket~~	~~bread~~	~~radio~~
~~socks~~	potatoes	spoon
~~boots~~	crisps	matches
~~t-shirt~~	bananas	cooking pot
hat	pizza	hook
~~trousers~~	biscuits	~~compass~~
bathing suit	~~oranges~~	~~knife~~

TOTAL POINTS: 17

When all the groups have read out their lists, students add up the items which have not been crossed off. They get one point for each unique item on their lists.

In groups, students then come up with reasons why it would be important to have these remaining items with them on the island and present their reasons to the class. The class votes on whether they agree with the group. If the class agrees with the reasons given, the group keeps the point. If not, the group loses the point for that item.

The winner is the group with the most points.

Variation:

This can be done with other vocabulary areas depending on the situation given.

e.g. *Pretend you are a teacher. Make lists of 5 things you want your students to bring to class.* [e.g.coursebook, pen etc] - *5 things you want them to be.* [e.g. adjectives – respectful, tidy etc] - *5 things you need in the class.* [e.g. chalk, desk etc].

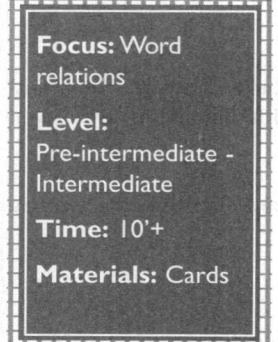

Concentration
(Pairs)

Photocopiable material: p. 171

Photocopiable material: p. 171

> ☞ **Pointer:**
>
> To avoid confusion, use only one lexical area in each game.

Focus: Word relations

Level: Pre-intermediate - Intermediate

Time: 10'+

Materials: Cards

Procedure:

Students play in pairs.
Prepare 20 paired word cards of the lexical area you wish to practise.

e.g. opposites: HOT COLD

present/past participles: HIDE HID

synonyms: UNUSUAL STRANGE

Give each pair of students the same paired cards. Students place the cards face down on the desk in a 5 x 4 layout.
Student A turns over any 2 cards and says both words.
If they match (e.g. the cards turned over are GOOD and BAD), student A takes both cards.
If they don't match (e.g. the cards turned over are HOT and BAD), student A puts back both cards, face down, in their original positions.
Student B repeats the procedure.
Students concentrate to remember the position of the revealed cards. In this way, if they pick up a new card, they must try to remember where the matching card is in order to win the pair.
The winner is the student with the most pairs of cards when all the matches have been made.

Sample cards:

WAKE	WOKE		HAPPY	SAD		BEGIN	START
MAKE	MADE		BEGIN	END		CRY	WEEP
GO	WENT		SWEET	SOUR		NEAT	TIDY

Variation:

Other lexical areas that may be practised.

Translations (for classes with the same mother tongue): e.g. HOUSE CASA

Words which take the same preposition: e.g. Believe in Interested in

Idiomatic expressions: e.g. The early bird catches the worm

Rhyme & Shout
(Pairs)

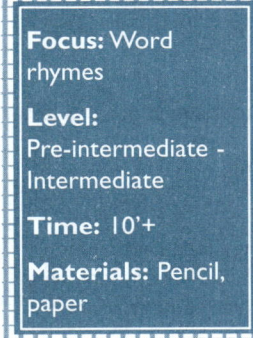

Focus: Word rhymes

Level: Pre-intermediate - Intermediate

Time: 10'+

Materials: Pencil, paper

Procedure:

Students play in pairs.

Student A writes down a word without letting student B see it. Student A then says a word that rhymes with their secret word. Student B must try to guess the secret word by saying words that rhyme with it. Student A notes how many attempts student B makes to find the word. Student B has up to 10 guesses and they get a point for each guess they use.

e.g.   Student A: (writes down pot): *It rhymes with lot.*
         Student B: *Got.*
         Student A: *No.*
         Student B: *Cot.*
         Student A: *No.*
         Student B: *Hot.*
         Student A: *No.*
         Student B: *Pot.*
         Student A: *Yes!*

Student B guessed the word after four guesses and gets four points. It is now student B's turn to write down a secret word. The winner is the student who has the least points after five rounds.

Variation:

For higher levels, students who are guessing the word do not just say rhyming words, but ask questions without saying the rhyming word they are thinking of.

e.g.   Student A: (writes down pot): *It rhymes with lot.*
         Student B: (thinking of got): *Does it mean something like had?*
         Student A: *No.*
         Student B: (thinking of cot): *Is it something you sleep on?*
         Student A: *No.*
         Student B: (thinking of hot): *Is it like the weather in summer?*
         Student A: *No.*
         Student B: (thinking of pot): *Can you use it for cooking?*
         Student A: *Yes!*

Student B scores four points. It is now student A's turn to guess the secret word.

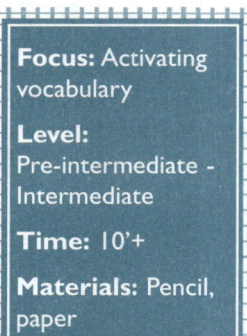

Word Squares
10 (Pairs)

Focus: Activating vocabulary

Level: Pre-intermediate - Intermediate

Time: 10'+

Materials: Pencil, paper

Procedure:

Students play in pairs.

Student A thinks of a 5 letter word and writes it down. e.g. FOUND.

Student B thinks of a word which starts with the first or last letter of FOUND to make another 5 letter word going down. e.g. FIGHT. Student A then does the same. e.g. adds THINK.

Student B finally has to find a word beginning with D and ending in K. e.g. DRINK.

e.g.

If a student cannot think of a word they lose that round. If the square is completed by student B, that student wins the round and thinks of a word to start the next round.

Associations
11 (Groups)

Photocopiable material: p. 172

Focus: Word associations

Level: Pre-Intermediate - Intermediate

Time: 15'+

Materials: Pencil, paper, toothpicks, cards

Procedure:

Students play in groups of three.

Give each student 5 toothpicks. Photocopy and give each group key word cards or have them make up their own.

Student A writes down a key word (or picks up a card) and two associated words without letting the others see.

(e.g. GOLD - ring, jewellery)

Student A tells the group the key word. Each of the other students has five guesses to come up with the two associated words.

For each wrong guess students lose a toothpick.

For each correct guess, students win a toothpick.

When the words have been guessed or the students have no guesses left, the students get another 5 toothpicks for the next round. (They add these to any toothpicks they have left.)

Student B then writes their key word and 2 associated words and the game continues.

The winner is the student with the most toothpicks after a designated number of rounds.

Sample Cards:

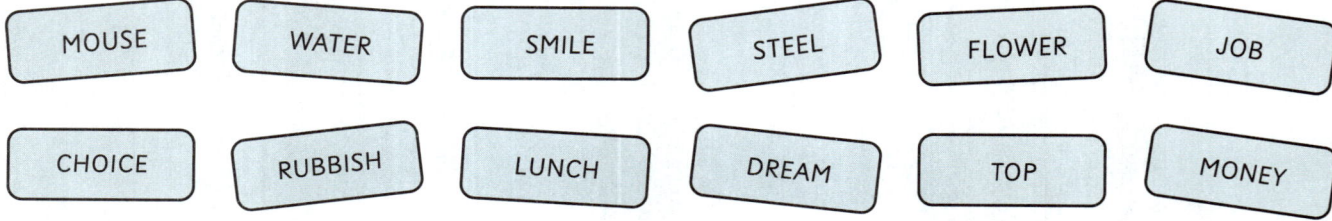

Noughts & Crosses – Tic-tac-toe

12 (Pairs)

Focus: Word relationships

Level: Pre-intermediate - Intermediate

Time: 15'+

Materials: Coloured pencils, paper

Procedure:

Students play in pairs.
Give each student a different coloured pencil and have them draw a 3x3 grid on a piece of paper.
Decide on a lexical area you wish to practise. e.g. adjectives, nouns, phrasal verbs, associated words, etc.

e.g. **Adjectives** - Make sure each student uses a different coloured pencil.
Student A begins by writing an adjective in a cell on the grid. e.g. sad
Student B must place a synonym or antonym to that word anywhere else on the grid. e.g. **happy**
Then student A writes a different adjective. Students try to block their opponent from getting three words in a line.
The winner is the first to complete a line of three cells, horizontally, diagonally or vertically.

e.g.
Student A: sad
Student B: **happy**
Student A: nice
Student B: **nasty**
Student A: pretty
Student B: **ugly**
Student A: big
Student B: **small**
Student B wins by having 3 in a row.

sad	**happy**	pretty
nice	big	
nasty	**ugly**	**small**

Alternatives:

1   Students make a grid and place words in each cell at random. Pairs trade grids with each other. Student A has to write antonyms and student B synonyms under the word in the cell they wish to go.

2   With more advanced levels, make the game more challenging by using a 4 x 4 grid.

3   Practice phrasal verbs or themes.
Phrasal verbs - Decide which particle/preposition to practise.
Students must place verbs in the cells which collate with the prepostition.
e.g. OUT - students may write: speak, leave, give, send, hand, etc.

Themes - Give students a theme. All the words used must be associated with this theme.
e.g. 'Things you can do with your mouth.' - students may write: gulp, shout, talk, drink, taste, chew, smile, etc.

Student A: gulp
Student B: **drink**
Student A: shout
Student B: **taste**
Student A: blow
Student B: **bite**
Student A: chew
Student A wins with 3 in a diagonal row.

gulp	**drink**		
shout	**bite**		
taste	chew		
		blow	

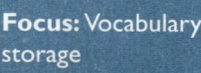

Warm Fuzzies & Cold Pricklies
13 (Groups)

Focus: Vocabulary storage

Level: Pre-intermediate - Intermediate

Time: 10'+

Materials: Pencil, paper

Procedure:

Students play in groups of three.

The aim is to revise vocabulary from a particular unit, text or topic area. Words/phrases are categorised into those the students like (Warm Fuzzies - ☺) and those they don't like (Cold Pricklies - ☹).

Photocopy a list of words or students find the words from their coursebooks.

Students may place the words/phrases under the headings as they please. They may choose to place them by the sound of the word, its perceived usefulness, memorability, difficulty, connotation or length.

e.g.

commute, delicious, chuckle, miserable, gorgeous, communicate, shake hands with, nasty, clap of thunder, Internet, uptight, nervous, fascinating, furious

WARM FUZZIES ☺	COLD PRICKLIES ☹
delicious	commute
chuckle	miserable
gorgeous	nasty
communicate	clap of thunder
shake hands with	uptight
Internet	nervous
fascinating	furious

When students have categorised the words, they share the reasons why they put the words under the headings with the rest of the group.

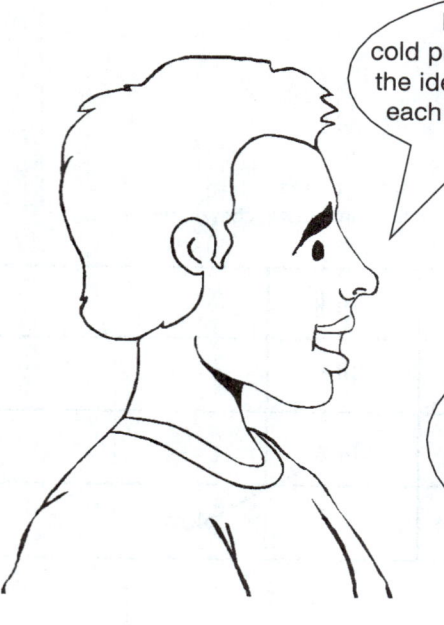

I put commute under cold pricklies because I don't like the idea of spending a long time each day in a crowded train or bus getting to work.

I put it under warm fuzzies because I like looking at all the different types of people and it gives me the chance to properly wake up before I get to work.

Switch
(Groups)

Photocopiable material: pp. 225-228

Focus: Lexical sets

Level: Pre-intermediate - Intermediate

Time: 15'+

Materials: Cards

Procedure:

Students play in groups of three.
Photocopy one set of 40 symbol cards for each group.
There are four symbol sets, each with ten cards numbered 1-10.
Choose subject areas to be represented by each symbol and write them on the board for reference.

e.g.   = clothes   = sports
         = jobs   = foods

The cards are shuffled and each student gets 7 cards. The rest are placed face down on the table.
The top card is turned over and placed face up beside these cards. (The number 1 card is considered a wild card and should not start the game.)
Students take it in turns to place cards on top of the starter card. The card each student puts down must match either the symbol or the number of the card already down. If a student does not have the same symbol or number as the card down but they have a wild card, they may put down the wild card and change the symbol to whatever they wish the next student to follow.
If a student cannot follow and does not have a wild card, they must pick up a card from the face down pack and add it to those in their hand. They keep picking up cards from the pack until they are able to put one down.
As students put down their cards, they must say a word that is related to the lexical set represented by the symbol on the card.

e.g.   **Starter card:** [7]   ⟶   Student A puts down [3] and says: *shirt.*

Student B puts down [3] and says: *pizza.*   Student C puts down [8] and says: *carrots.*

Student A puts down [1] and says: *change symbol to ball* (sports) - *tennis.*

Student B has no cards and no wild cards, so picks up from the face down pile until they get a card they can put down.

The game continues in this way until one student has put down all their cards or nobody can continue.

The students add up the points in their hand (1 point for each card) and keep track on a piece of paper.
The winner is the student who has the fewest points after a set number of rounds.

Giddy Stick

15 (Pairs)

Photocopiable material: pp. 173-174

Focus: Lexical sets

Level: Pre-intermediate - Intermediate

Time: 15'+

Materials: Board, counters, cards, letter tiles, die/spinner

Pointers:

- Use **categories** which relate to students' knowledge and interests.
- At higher levels, students say three things that begin with the chosen letter.

Procedure:

Students play in pairs.

Photocopy and give each student their own board and two counters. Give each pair a set of letter tiles, category cards and a die/spinner. Students shuffle and place the letter tiles and cards face down in two piles next to the boards and their counters in the start position in the bottom left corner of their boards.

Each student takes 12 letter tiles which they place in the ascending and descending spaces on their board. Students take it in turns to roll the die/spin the spinner to move up the rungs of the board and answer questions based on the category cards. If the student answers correctly, they stay where they are. If not, they go back to the start position and it is the other student's turn to play.

In order to reach the middle circle and move to the descending rungs, a student must roll/spin the exact number needed to land there.

e.g. If a student is on the 5th rung, they must roll/spin a two to get to the middle and therefore move to the descending column. At this point, if the student has not rolled/spun the exact number, they have the option of moving their counter back that number of spaces or moving their second counter forward.

e.g. Student A: Rolls/spins 5 and lands on S
Student B: Picks up a category card. *The subject is furniture. What piece of furniture begins with S?*
Student A: *Sofa.* (Student A remains on rung 5 and it is now student B's turn to roll/spin.)
Student B: Rolls/spins 4 and lands on G.
Student A: Picks up a category card. *The subject is music. What musical instrument begins with G?*
Student B: Can't think of anything and returns to the start postion.

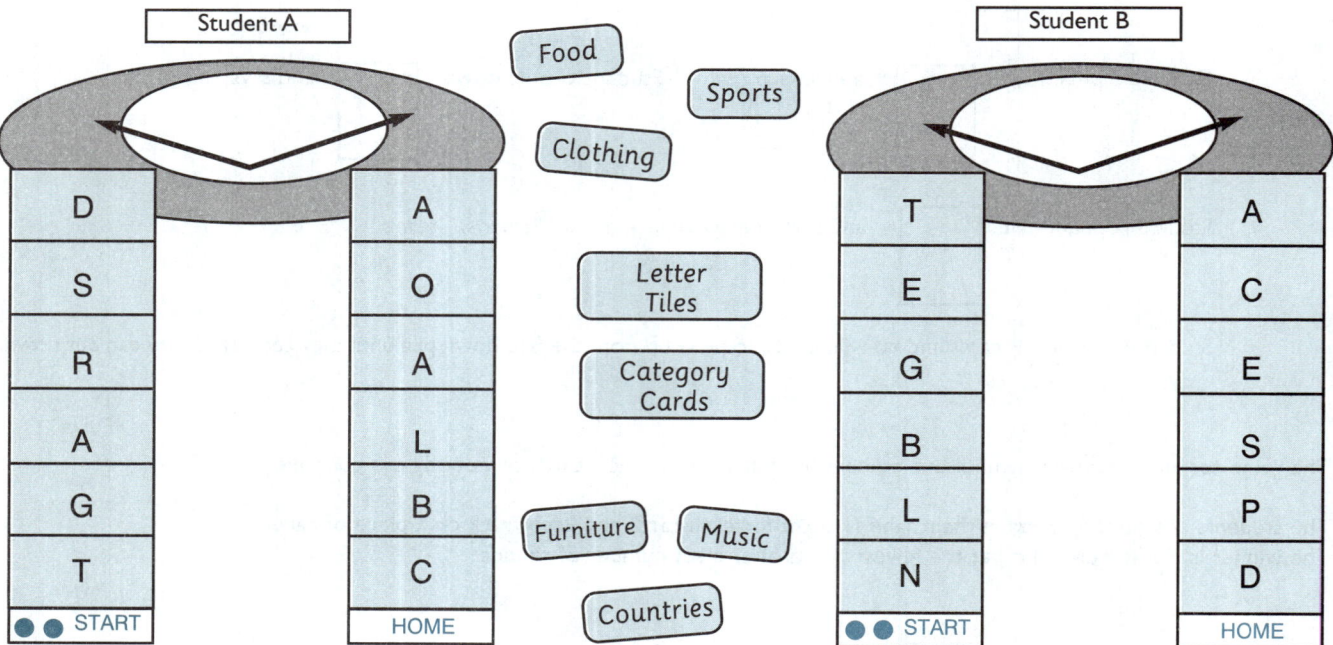

Extension:

For higher levels, when a student lands on a letter, the other student picks a category card and asks for three words beginning with that letter.

Word Segments
(Pairs)

Photocopiable material: pp. 175, 229-231

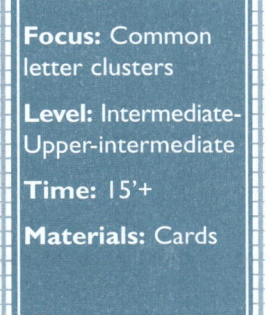

Focus: Common letter clusters

Level: Intermediate-Upper-intermediate

Time: 15'+

Materials: Cards

Procedure:

Students play in pairs.
Photocopy or have students prepare common letter cluster cards and single letter cards.
The cards are shuffled and each student receives 3 cluster cards, 2 letter cards and 5 blank cards.
Students take it in turns to make a word of at least four letters using the cards they have.
Each word must include at least one cluster or single letter card, but not more than one of each type.
Students may write two to three letters on each blank card, at any point in the game.
A student can add any of their cards to a word formed by another student if it extends that word.
The winner is the one who puts down all their cards first.
The cards are now reshuffled and a new game begins.

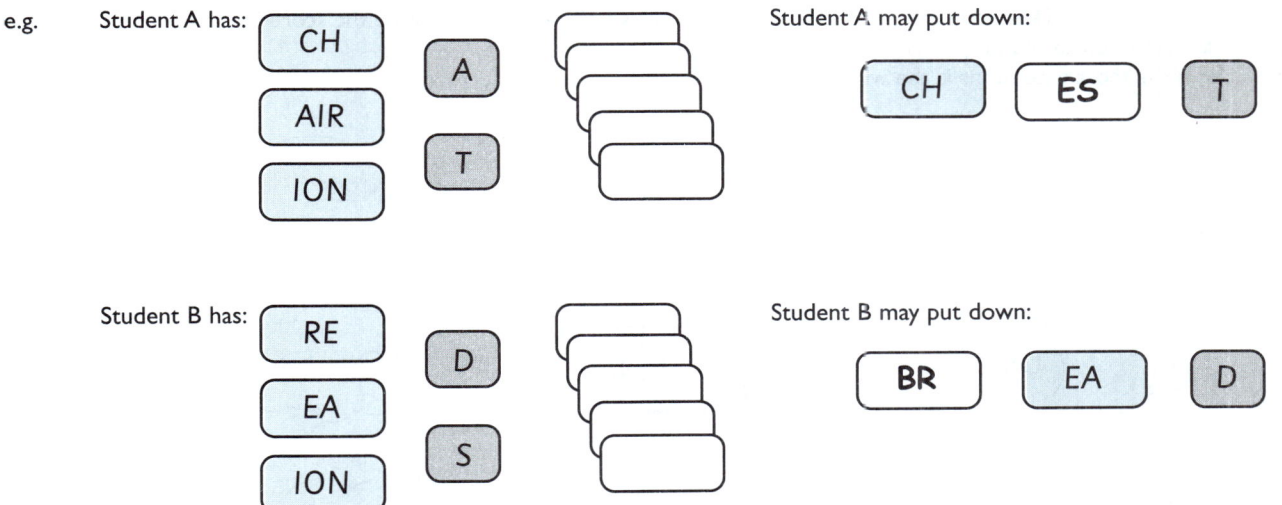

Student B can also put the S card they have at the end of student A's word, making it CHESTS.
Students should try not to use up their cluster or single letter cards too quickly as they need at least one for each word they form.

Sample Cards:

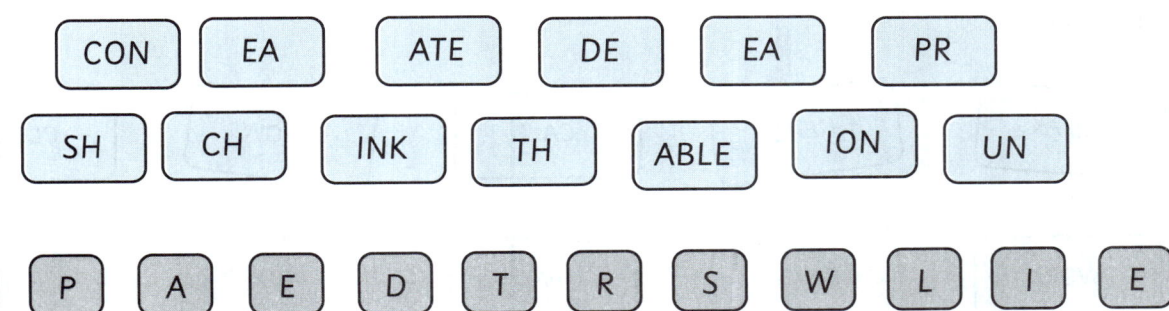

Spidergram
(Groups)

Photocopiable material: p. 176

Focus: Vocabulary expansion, lexical fields

Level: Intermediate-Upper-intermediate

Time: 15'+

Materials: Cards, pencil, paper

Procedure:

Students play in groups of three.

Give each group the same root word card or dictate a root word to the class.

Each group chooses a student to be the secretary.

The students have 1 minute to come up with as many extensions to the root word as they can.

e.g. collocations, adding affixes, phrases with the root word, etc.

The secretary writes these down and also participates in the game.

When the minute is up, group secretaries swap papers.

The secretary for group A reads out the expansions on the paper in front of them. Each of the secretaries puts a tick next to the extensions they hear.

When the secretary for group A has finished reading all the extensions on the paper they have, the other group secretaries take it in turns to read out any extensions that have not been read out.

The secretaries count the number of ticks on the paper and write the score at the bottom.

The papers are returned to the original group.

The group with the most extensions is the winner.

e.g.

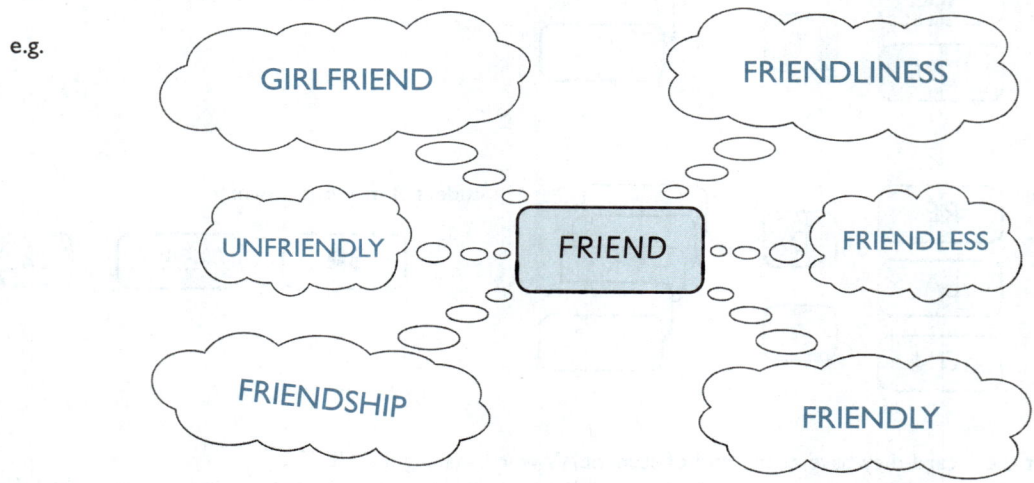

With higher levels expressions and idioms may be accepted.

e.g. fairweather friend, a friend in need is a friend indeed, etc.

Sample Cards:

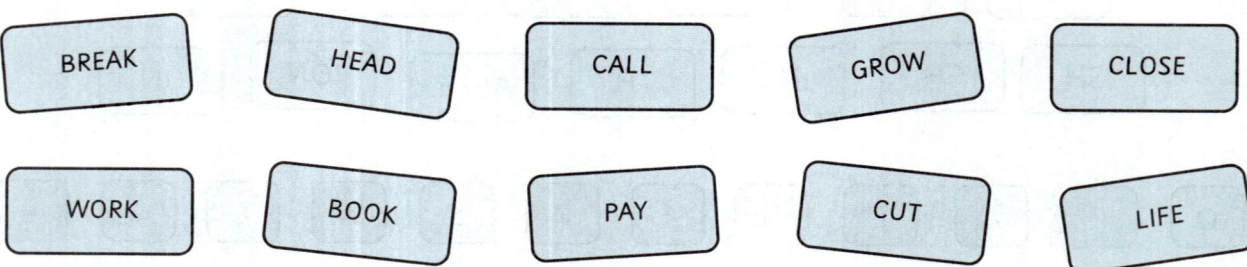

Word Grid
(Pairs)

18

☞ **Pointer:**

Alter the size of grids to suit the level of your students. Lower levels might use a 4 x 4 grid.

Focus: Spelling, vocabulary activation

Level: Intermediate

Time: 15'+

Materials: Pencil, paper

Procedure:

Students play in pairs.
Each student draws a 5x5 grid on a piece of paper.
Students take it in turns to call out letters which they write on their grids anywhere they want.

The aim is to make as many five-letter words as possible, reading across or down in any direction (left to right or right to left).

e.g.   Student A begins by saying a letter and writing it on their gird wherever they want.
Student B also writes this letter anywhere on their grid. Then, student B says a letter and both students write it on their grid. Letters can be repeated at any time.

Student A

e				
t				l
h				

Student B

	l	e		
h				
			t	

Helpful Hints

When each letter is called out, students should think of where they could best place it to help them form words.
The more common letters that begin or end words should be put in the outside spaces.

Students continue to call out letters until the grids are full. Each student then counts the number of words they have formed. The student with the most words is the winner.

e.g.

Student A

e	o	m	c	s
t	n	o	l	l
e	r	r	a	e
s	h	a	p	e
h	e	l	s	p

Student B

s	l	e	e	p
h	e	a	r	s
e	c	m	h	a
e	n	r	o	l
p	l	o	t	s

Student A has formed 4 words. Student B has formed 5 words and wins this round.

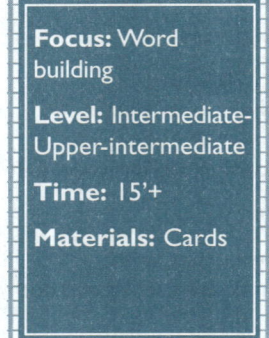

Word Building Dominoes
(Pairs)

Photocopiable material: pp. 177-178

Focus: Word building

Level: Intermediate-Upper-intermediate

Time: 15'+

Materials: Cards

Procedure:

Students play in pairs.

Photocopy or have students prepare domino cards and root word cards. The domino cards have a prefix written on the right and a suffix on the left. The root word cards have words which can be expanded by adding a suffix or prefix. The same suffix and prefix may be written on several different cards.

Give each student 10 domino cards and ten root word cards.

Give each pair one additional root word card to start the game. This card is placed face up on the table.

Students take it in turns to add domino cards and root word cards to make a chain.

A suffix added to the root word does not have to make sense with the prefix already down.

e.g. The root word is LIKE. Student A puts down OUS/DIS to make DISLIKE. Student B puts down LY/UN to make LIKELY.

Students may add suffixes to root words ending in E or Y where a spelling change is necessary.

e.g.

A student who adds a root word card to a prefix that does not make sense, must also add a suffix to complete it properly.

e.g. After student B put down LY/UN to make LIKELY, student A put down the root word card THINK and then added ABLE/CON to get UNTHINKABLE.

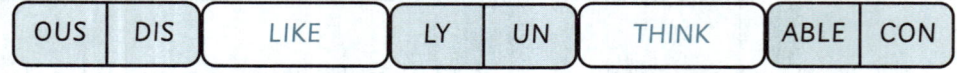

If a student cannot put down a root word or domino card, they miss a turn. The winner is the first student to use all their cards.

Variation:

Students play in groups of three.

Have students make 30 compound noun domino cards and then cut them up into the individual words.

The cards are shuffled and each student gets 10 cards. Student A starts by placing a card on the table. Student B must now place a card before or after to make a compound noun. If student B does not have a match, it is student C's turn.

e.g.

The student who finds the match, restarts the game with another card from their hand.

Topic Types
20 (Groups)

Photocopiable material: pp. 179, 229-231

Focus: Lexical sets

Level: Intermediate

Time: 15'+

Materials: Board, counters, die/spinner, letter tiles

Procedure:

Students play in groups of three.

Photocopy and give each group a copy of the board, a bag/envelope of letter tiles, a die/spinner and counters.

Choose six topic areas you wish to practise. Tell groups to write them in the six blank spaces provided at the top of the board in the order you say them.

e.g. 1-animals, 2-food, 3-jobs, 4-transport, 5-emotions, 6-sports

Each student places a counter in their own start box.

Students take it in turns to roll/spin and match the number to the topic at the top of the board. Then they take four letter tiles from the bag/envelope.

The student whose turn it is must now think of four words, beginning with these letters, related to the topic and give a definition for each one.

If successful, the student rolls/spins again and moves that number of spaces.

If the student lands on a **?**, they must answer one question from each of the other students in the group about their topic.

If they give acceptable answers, they stay where they are. If not, they move back to their original position.

Students move around the squares on the outside of the board until they come back to their own starting area, where they move up the grey squares to the home position.

The first student to go around the board and reach home is the winner.

1 animals	2 food	3 jobs	4 transport	5 emotions	6 sports

e.g.

Student A rolls/spins 3 - topic will be jobs.

Student A takes four letters: **F, I, O, T.**

Student A: *F is for farmer who grows things for food.*

I is for inspector who checks that everything is as it should be.

O is for optician who examines our eyes.

T is for teacher who tries to educate us.

Student A now rolls/spins 6, and lands on a **?**.

Student B: *What is the best job and why?*

Student A: *The best job is to be a doctor because you help people who are ill get better.*

Student C: *Is money the most important thing in a job?*

Student A: *Money is important but I think it's better to do something that you enjoy and makes you happy.*

Student B and C accept the answers and student A stays where they are. It is now student B's turn to play.

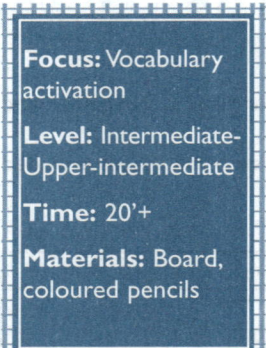

Battleships
(Pairs)

Photocopiable material: p. 180

Focus: Vocabulary activation

Level: Intermediate-Upper-intermediate

Time: 20'+

Materials: Board, coloured pencils

Procedure:

Students play in pairs.

Photocopy and give each student a 14x5 grid.

There are four types of '*battleships*': noun, adjective, verb and three-word phrases (verb+adjective+noun). Each 'battleship' covers one square. Each student places their 'battleships' at random on the grid by writing the letter **N** - noun, **A** - adjective, **V** - verb and **P** - three-word phrase, five times for each one. Students play facing each other with a large book or file upright on the table between them so they cannot see the other student's grid.

Students take it in turns to call out grid references to try and locate the other student's 'battleships'. Each time a student calls out a grid reference they put a tick in that cell to remember that they have called it out. If student A calls out a grid reference and student B does not have a 'battleship' in that cell, student B says '*Miss*'. If student A calls out a reference and student B has a 'battleship' in that cell, then student B says '*Hit!*' and what type of 'battleship' it is. Student A must now say a word of the type of 'battleship' they hit, beginning with the letter of the cell the word covers. If successful, student B draws a line through the cell indicating that the 'battleship' was sunk.

e.g. Student A: *H2.*
Student B: *Miss. M5.*
Student A: *Miss. C4*
Student B: *Hit! Noun.*
Student A: *Crocodile.*

e.g. Student B: *R1*
Student A: *Miss.G4.*
Student B: *Miss. E5*
Student A: *Hit! Three-word phrase.*
Student B: *Eat enormous eggs.*

Sample board: (for student B)

	A	B	C	D	E	F	G	H	L	M	N	R	S	T
1	N		✓			A		V			P			N
2		V		P				✓	P		A			
3					P	N			A	V			P	
4	V		N				✓		N					
5		A			A								V	

N - noun   A - adjective   P - 3 word phrase   V - verb

X-word
22 (Pairs)

Focus: Lexical sets, general knowledge

Level: Intermediate-Upper-intermediate

Time: 10'+

Materials: Pencil, paper

Procedure:

Students play in pairs.

Write various categories on the board (e.g. cities, sports, food, etc).

In pairs, students choose a category and then take it in turns to write down words related to that theme.

As the students say the word, they must say one fact they know about that word.

Each word written down, after the first one, must use a letter of a word already written down.

e.g. Theme: Places

Student A: *Manchester. It has the richest football team in the world.*
Student B: *Madrid. It is the capital of Spain.*
Student A: *Tokyo. It is the biggest city in Japan.*
Student B: *India. It has the second largest population in the world.*　　**etc**

```
M A N C H E S T E R
A                 O
D                 K
R                 Y
I N D I A         O
D
```

e.g.　Theme: Fruit & vegetables

Student A: *Cantaloupe. It is orange inside.*
Student B: *Eggplant. It is usually purple on the outside.*
Student A: *Cucumber. We use cucumbers in salad.*
Student B: *Tomato. Tomatoes are very good for you and have lots of vitamins.*　　**etc**

```
C A N T A L O U P E
U               G
C               G
U               P
M               L
B               A
E               N
R A D I S H     T O M A T O
```

The game continues until nobody can add a word using the spaces available.

The winner is the student who has written and said something about the most words on the chosen category.

In Other Words
(Pairs)

Photocopiable material: p. 181

Focus: Word guessing

Level: Intermediate

Time: 15'+

Materials: Cards

Procedure:

Students play in pairs.

Give some examples of kennings to the students.

Prepare or have students make 10 noun word cards each. Each card will have the noun word at the top and a description or kenning written under it. The cards are placed in the centre of the desk.

Students take it in turns to read out their description/kenning to the other student. Each student has three guesses to find the correct noun. Students get one point for each correct guess. If a student does not find the word after three guesses the card goes to the bottom of the pile.

The winner is the one with the most points at the end of the game.

e.g. Student A: | CAT
rat catcher | *Rat catcher.*

Student B: *Trap.*
Student A: *No.*
Student B: *Cheese.*
Student A: *No.*
Student B: *Cat.*
Student A: *Yes!*

> This activity is based on *Kennings.*
> A kenning is a phrase which describes something without using its name. It is common in Old Norse and Old English poetry.
> e.g. a helmet might be a 'head protector'.

Sample Cards:

FORK
food lifter

ELECTRICITY
light giver

FOOD
stomach filler

CAR
gas guzzler

BABY
cot screamer

HAIR
head warmer

GLUE
paper sticker

BAG
book carrier

SUN
heat provider

ICE
drink cooler

CAT
rat catcher

SHOE
foot supporter

Snake Lotto
(Groups)

Photocopiable material: pp. 229-231

Focus: Spelling, word building

Level: Intermediate

Time: 15+

Materials: Letter tiles

Procedure:

Students play in groups of three.
Give each group an envelope/bag of 25 letter tiles.
Students arrange the letter tiles randomly in a 5 x 5 grid.
Students have 3 minutes to write down as many words as they can that can be formed from the letter tiles. The letters making the words must be touching horizontally, vertically or diagonally in any direction. A letter may be used twice in one word or in more than one word.

e.g.

A	V	G	S	O
F	B	P	E	L
R	A	E	T	T
S	D	M	N	A
I	F	D	H	U

Possible words: RAM, SETTLE, HAT, BEE, TEAR, DRAPES, etc.

The winner is the student who finds the most words in the set time.

Variation:

Choose the letter for the centre square in advance. This letter should be a vowel and must be included in all words.

e.g. From the above square, where the central letter is E, students may find the following words:

BED, DENT, NEAR, EAR, EARS, MEET, MEN, EEL, MEND, SPEND, etc.

Alternative:

Students play in groups of three.
Give each group a complete set of letter tiles in an envelope/bag. Each student takes 10 letter tiles which they place face up in front of them. Students must try to use as many of their letter tiles as possible to make words.

e.g. Student A has: BESEURAJIT and rearranges the letter to make:

SURE JAB TIE

Student A has used all 10 letters and scores 10 points.

Student B has: FRAMELONGI and rearranges the letters to make:

GAIN FOR ME

Student B has used only 9 letters and scores 9 points.

After each round the letter tiles are put back into the envelope/bag and a new round begins.
The winner is the student with the most points after 3 rounds.

Picture this!
25 (Groups)

Photocopiable material: p.182

Focus: Describing things

Level: Intermediate

Time: 20'+

Materials: Cards, die/spinner, pencil, paper

Procedure:

Students play in groups of three. Two groups play against each other.
Photocopy or have students make sets of category cards.
Shuffle the cards and give each group 10 cards and a die/spinner.
Each card has 4 categories (of your choosing) on it.

e.g
- Person/place/animal = **P**
- Object [something you can touch or see] = **O**
- Action [something you can do] = **A**
- Qualities/ideas/feelings [e.g. happiness/life/soft] = **Q**

Each category corresponds to a number 1 - 4.   e.g. P-1, O-2, A-3, Q-4

A student from group A picks up a card without showing it to the others and rolls the die/spins the spinner to decide on the category. If the student rolls/spins a 5 or 6, the turn goes to the next student in the group. If the student rolls/spins a 1, 2, 3, or 4, the student tells the group the category and then draws what is on the card. The rest of the group try to guess the word that the sketch represents. Each group has a minute to find the word. If they guess correctly, they keep the card. If not, group B has a chance to guess and take that card. If neither of the teams can guess, the card is placed at the bottom of the pile and play goes to group B.
The group with the most cards after a designated number of rounds wins.

Alternative:

Students define the word, without saying it, or mime it rather than draw it.
This leads to more language activation and a faster and more interactive game.

Sample Cards:

1 - P CAPTAIN 2 - O POT 3 - A TICKLE 4 - Q FURRY	1 - P LIFEGUARD 2 - O PIN 3 - A EXPLAIN 4 - Q BRIGHT

1 - P ANT 2 - O BOX 3 - A ARGUE 4 - Q GENTLE	1 - P ROME 2 - O LAMP 3 - A JUMP 4 - Q LIFE

1 - P BABY 2 - O WINDOW 3 - A FALL 4 - Q JOY	1 - P PARROT 2 - O VIOLIN 3 - A GRAB 4 - Q TASTY

1 - P GIANT 2 - O SHELF 3 - A EXTEND 4 - Q TIDY	1 - P HOME 2 - O DIAMOND 3 - A ACCELERATE 4 - Q POOR

26 Don't Mention It!
(Groups)

Photocopiable material: p. 183

Focus: Definitions

Level: Intermediate-Upper-intermediate

Time: 15'+

Materials: Cards

Procedure:

Students play in groups of at least four. Two groups play against each other.
Photocopy or prepare sets of cards which have a main word and 4 associated words under it.
Give each two groups 20 cards. The cards are shuffled and placed faced down between the groups.
Student A from group A picks up a card and tries to get their group to come up with the main word on the card - the word at the top- without saying any of the associated words underneath. A student from the other group looks over student A's shoulder to make sure they do not use any of the associated words.
If group A guesses the word, they keep that card. If not, or student A says any of the associated words, group B gets the card.
The aim is to elicit as many of the main words as possible in a certain time (1 or 2 minutes).
Once the time is up, it is the next group's turn. Each student has a turn at being the elicitor.
The group with the most cards at the end of the game is the winner.

Sample Cards:

BRIGHT	MAP	HUMAN	EARTH
LIGHT	DIRECTIONS	ANIMAL	PLANET
SUN	GUIDE	PEOPLE	MOON
DULL	CHART	WE	SPACE
CLEVER	PLACES	BEING	WORLD

27 Red Letter
(Groups)

Photocopiable material: pp. 184, 229-231

Focus: Vocabulary activation

Level: Intermediate

Time: 10'+

Materials: Grid, letter tiles

Procedure:

Students play in groups of three.
Photocopy or have each student prepare a grid with headings of your choosing at the top.
Each group takes a letter tile from a bag/envelope.
Students try to come up with words beginning with the chosen letter that fit under each heading.
The round is over after one minute or when one student in the group has completed the row.
Students take it in turns to read out the words on their grids.
Each word under a correct heading gets 5 points.
If a student has a word under a heading that no one else has, they get 10 points for that word.
The winner is the student with the most points after five rounds.

Sample Grid: Letter tile: A

Name - male	Name - female	Country	Things in the home	Plant	Animal	Job
Arthur	Anna	Austria	armchair	artichoke	ant	artist

A Good Match

28 (Groups)

Photocopiable material: p. 185

Focus: Collocations

Level: Intermediate - Advanced

Time: 15'+

Materials: Cards

Procedure:

Students play in groups of three.
Prepare cards using high frequency verbs and collocating adjectives with noun cards.

e.g.
| BREAK | NEW | GROUND |

These may be recently learned vocabulary items.
Give each group a set of cards with an equal number of verbs, adjectives and nouns. The cards are shuffled and each student gets the same number of cards.
Students take it in turns to look at their cards and put down as many acceptable collocations as they can making sure the cards are in the order: verb + adjective + noun.

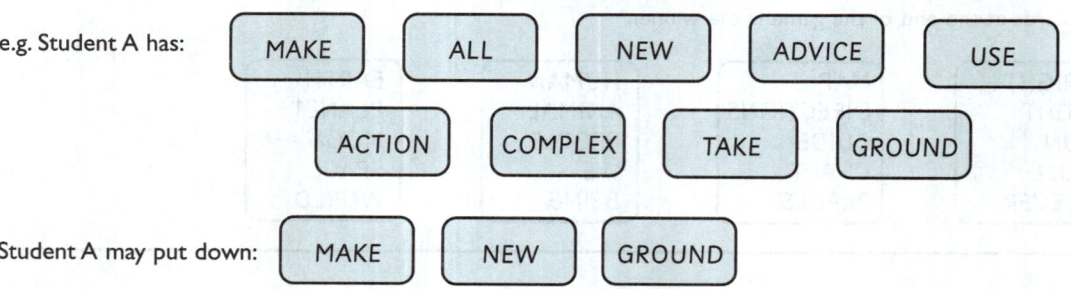

e.g. Student A has: | MAKE | ALL | NEW | ADVICE | USE |
| ACTION | COMPLEX | TAKE | GROUND |

Student A may put down: | MAKE | NEW | GROUND |

It is not the original collocation, but it is acceptable providing student A can explain the meaning.
When all the students have put down as many sets as they can, they decide from the cards they have left in their hand what word or words they need to complete a collocation set.
In order to get the word or words they require, students take turns to - **1)** look at the cards the other students have put down to see whether they can exchange a word in their hand for one that is down, or **2)** call out a word they need and if another student has it, they pass it to them.

e.g. Student B still has: | MISTAKE | BREAK | SERIOUS |

Student B may exchange | BREAK | with | MAKE | from student A and put down: MAKE SERIOUS MISTAKE.

Sample cards:

Verbs	Adjectives	Nouns
FIND	COMPLEX	RESOURCES
FOLLOW	RELEVANT	EXAMPLES
GIVE	APPROPRIATE	PROCEDURES
TAKE	NEW	ACTION

Give Me 5!
(Pairs)

Photocopiable material: pp. 186, 225-228

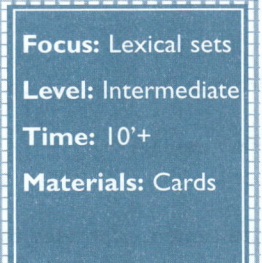

Focus: Lexical sets

Level: Intermediate

Time: 10'+

Materials: Cards

Procedure:

Students play in pairs.
Prepare task cards based on lexical sets – at least 20 cards for each pair.
Photocopy three symbol card sets (with different symbols), each set numbered 1-10.
Give each pair 20 task cards and three symbol card sets

The task cards are placed face down on the table.
Student A takes one set of symbol cards and student B another. Both students place the sets face down in front of them. The third set is placed face down in the centre of the table.
The top card from the central pile is turned face up and placed next to the pile.
Both students turn over their top card and place them down next to their piles.

Students can earn the chance to answer a question and win a task card if:
1. They have a higher numbered card than the other student.
2. They have a lower numbered card but it is the same number as the starter card.
(If all three cards are the same number, they are put to one side and a new card from the central pile is turned face up.)

e.g. Student A:    Starter Card:    Student B:

Student A has the higher numbered card. Student B picks up a task card and asks student A to complete the task. If student A completes the task succesfully they get that card.

e.g. **Task card:**

   Student B: *Tell me the names of five pieces of furniture.*
   Student A: *Bed, table, chair, sofa, desk.*

The student with the most task cards at the end of the game is the winner.

Sample Cards:

5 countries beginning with A

5 types of furniture

5 types of jewellery

5 girls' names with one syllable

5 facial expressions

5 means of transport

5 activities you can do in the sea

5 good qualities

5 outdoor jobs

5 wild animals

5 vegetarian foods

5 bad habits

It's So Common
30 (Pairs)

☞ **Pointer:**

Use blue and red pens to write instead of grey and white cards.

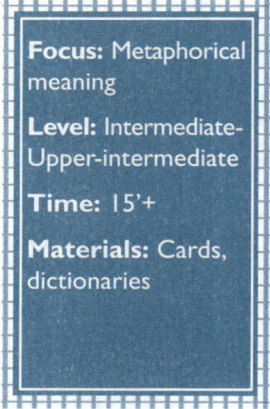

Focus: Metaphorical meaning

Level: Intermediate-Upper-intermediate

Time: 15'+

Materials: Cards, dictionaries

Procedure:

Students play in pairs.
Give each pair a monolingual dictionary, 3 white and 3 grey cards, and one verb that they will look up.

Pairs use the dictionaries to write sentences using common verbs with multiple meanings.
e.g. do, get, give, have, keep, look, make, put, take, know, etc.

Pairs choose 3 example uses for their verb and, on the WHITE cards, write sentences/phrases to illustrate these uses. Then, on the GREY cards, they write a sentence which could follow the sentence/phrase to exemplify the meaning.

e.g.   Pair A: Has the verb 'give'.

White cards:

Give me a break! | Give it your best shot. | He gave away my secret.

Grey cards:

You're always yelling at me! | I knew you could do it! | I can't trust him anymore.

Collect the cards in separate piles (white and grey) from all the pairs and mix them up. Redistribute the cards so that every pair again has 3 white and 3 grey cards which they put face up in front of them.

Pair A starts by reading out one of their white cards to the class. If another pair thinks they have a matching grey card they read it out to the class. If the class agrees that the combination is correct, then pair A gives the white card to the other pair and they turn both cards face down. It is now that pair's turn to read out one of their white cards.

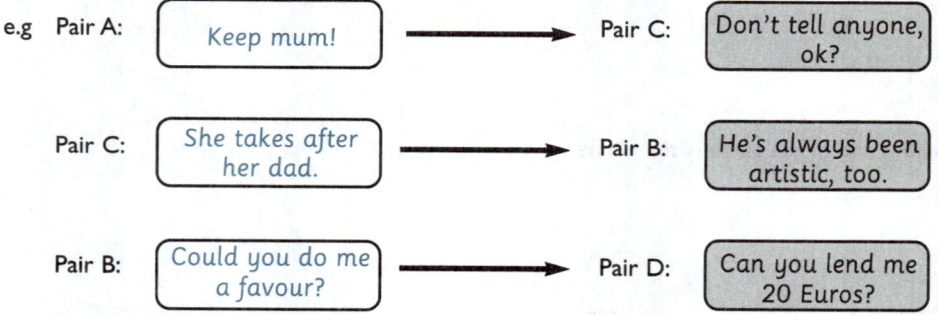

e.g   Pair A: Keep mum!   ⟶   Pair C: Don't tell anyone, ok?

Pair C: She takes after her dad.   ⟶   Pair B: He's always been artistic, too.

Pair B: Could you do me a favour?   ⟶   Pair D: Can you lend me 20 Euros?

The winner is the first pair to turn all their cards face down.

What are they like?
(Groups)

Photocopiable material: p. 187

Focus: Collocations, adjectives

Level: Upper-intermediate - Advanced

Time: 15'+

Materials: Cards, dictionaries

Procedure:

Students play in groups of three.
Each group prepares a list of 15 compound adjectives. e.g well-worded Each word is written on a separate card. Students may use dictionaries to make their lists. Each group also makes a board with three columns and 15 rows where they will place the cards.
The cards from each group are mixed up and given to another group.
Each student receives 10 cards.

Individually, students sort their cards into as many compounds as they can.
They place the compounds in the first two spaces on the board and in the third space, write a noun that could fit to complete the expression.

When students have put down as many compounds as they can, they take it in turns to put down one of their remaining cards in the correct column and the person to the right sees if they have an appropriate collocation.
If they do, they put it down and write in a noun. If not, they put down one of their spare cards in the correct column. If a student cannot think of a noun to complete the collocation, they cannot put down their card.
The student who puts down all their cards first is the winner.

e.g. Student A: | well | Student B: | worded | and writes: *letter*

Sample collocations:

short	lived	success
closely	guarded	secret
kind	hearted	man
long	winded	discussion
happily	married	couple
brightly	painted	room

4 Grammar

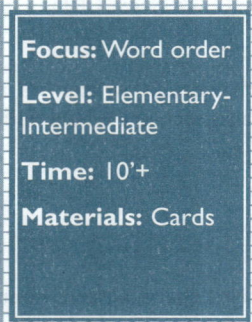

Sentence Generator
1 (Pairs)

☞ **Pointer:**

For more advanced levels, increase the number of words used.

Focus: Word order

Level: Elementary-Intermediate

Time: 10'+

Materials: Cards

Procedure:

Students play in pairs.

Each pair thinks of a sentence with a minimum of four words and writes each word on a separate card. The cards are shuffled so that the words are not in the original order.

Pairs swap cards and then have to place the cards they receive in what they think was the original order.

e.g.

| like | bike | to | my | I | school | riding |

becomes:

| I | like | riding | my | bike | to | school |

Pairs get 1 point for a correct sentence.
Allow students 30 seconds to put the words in order and check if they are correct.
After five turns the team with the most points wins.

Variation:

Students prepare sentences as above. Before passing the cards to the next pair, one card is removed
The pair receiving the cards has to guess what the missing word is and where it goes in the sentence.

e.g.

| stormy | it | a | night | was | and |

becomes:

| it | was | a | dark | and | stormy | night |

Give two points here. One for spotting the missing word and the other for putting the sentence in the correct order.

You're So Far Away From Me
(Groups)

2

Focus: Question forms

Level: Elementary-Intermediate

Time: 10'+

Materials: Questionnaire

Procedure:

Divide the class into two groups.

Prepare and hand out a questionnaire form to each student.

Students in each group ask each other questions to fill in the questionnaire and find out who they are most similar to.

Students use full question and answer forms.

e.g. Student A: *What's your favourite colour?*
      Student B: *My favourite colour is brown.*
      Student A: *What's your hardest school subject?*
      Student B: *My hardest subject is maths.*

	Me	Mark	Susan	Laura	Paul
Favourite colour	green	brown	green	blue	green
Hardest school subject	geography	maths	history	geography	French
Best holiday	skiing	beach	skiing	camping	beach
Favourite song					
Favourite animal					
Favourite food					

Students tell the rest of the class who they think they are most similar to and why.

For higher levels, use more abstract ideas:

Idea of the perfect evening
Idea of happiness
Future ambitions
Country you would most like to visit and why
Safest means of transport
Best book you've ever read
Best film you've ever seen
Best meal you've ever eaten
Job you'd most like
Person you'd most like to meet
Best present you've ever received

At all levels, encourage students to add their own ideas.

Get in line
(Groups)

Photocopiable material: pp. 188, 229-231

Focus: Story telling, past tenses, adjectives

Level: Pre-intermediate - Intermediate

Time: 10'+

Materials: Cards, letter tiles

Procedure:

Students play in groups of three.

Give each group a bag/envelope of letter tiles and a set of story start cards face down.

Each student takes ten letter tiles and places them face up in front of them.

Student A turns over a start card and reads it to the group.

Student A has to continue the story by adding a sentence containing one adjective and one verb beginning with letters on their letter tiles. Student A puts down these tiles next to the start card as they say the continuation to the story.

The continuation may contain more than one adjective or verb, but only two letter tiles can be put down in any turn. Student B and student C continue in the same way.

The winner is the first to put down all their letter tiles. If a student cannot think of an adjective and/or verb beginning with their letters, they lose a turn.

e.g. Student A has the letters:

Student A: | The light came on suddenly... |

He woke up immediately and saw a large man by the door.

Alternative:

Letters have to be used in alphabetical order. Any student in a group can put down a letter tile if they have the next in sequence. This version makes the outcome more random.

Sample Cards:

A poor boy went to market to sell the family cow.

He thought he had a job for life, but...

Sam was my pet...

If only she had stayed at home that day...

The light came on suddenly...

The world had changed completely.

Once upon a time there was a ...

It was a dark and stormy night...

Yesterday was the happiest day of my life.

My friend Peter liked to help other people.

He should never have answered the telephone that day.

As I was walking down the street, ...

Moral Maze
(Groups)

Photocopiable material: pp. 189-190

Focus: Decision making

Level: Pre-intermediate - Intermediate

Time: 15'+

Materials: Cards, board, die/spinner, counters

Procedure:

Students play in groups of three. Two groups play against each other.
Give each two groups a maze board, two counters and a set of 12 situation cards, placed face down.
Each group places their counter in the centre of the maze.
Groups turn the spinner/throw the die to see how many spaces they move each time.
Where there is a space in the maze wall they can choose to proceed through it.

If group A lands on a white space their turn stops and it is group B's turn.
If group A lands on a shaded space, group B picks up a situation card and reads out the question to group A, but not the options.
The students in group A discuss the question and decide what they would do. If their decision matches any of the three options, group B asks for a reason for their decision. If acceptable, group A gets the card. Group A throws/spins again and advances. If they land on a shaded space, they move one space forwards or backwards, as they wish. It is now group B's turn.
The winner is the group with the most cards when they have all been used.

e.g. **Card:**

> What would you do if you found a lot of money left on a seat in a bus?
> A   Keep it.
> B   Give it to the driver.
> C   Take it to the police station.

Group B: *What would you do if you found a lot of money left on a seat in a bus?*
Group A: *If we found money left on a seat in a bus, we would give it to the driver.*
Group B: *Why?*
Group A: *We would give it to the driver because the person who forgot it might come back to look for it.*

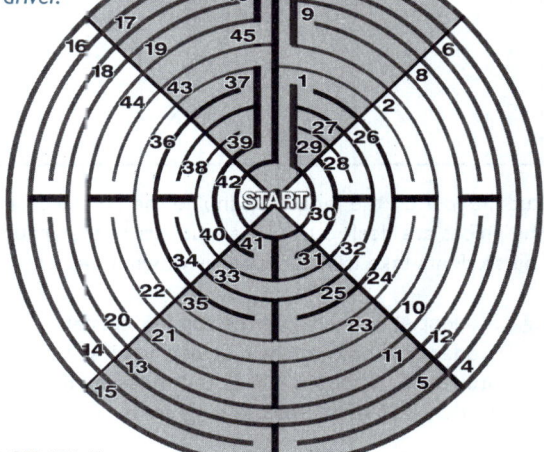

Extension:

Students prepare situation cards to practise different structures.
(The photocopiable material practises hypothetical situations.)

Sample Cards:

GOING TO

> Your best friend forgets your birthday. What are you going to do?
> A   Say nothing.
> B   Tell her you're upset with her.
> C   Not buy her a present when it is her birthday.

PAST SIMPLE

> You didn't do your homework. What do you say to the teacher?
> A   I left it at home.
> B   The dog ate it.
> C   It was too boring but if you want I'll do it for the next lesson.

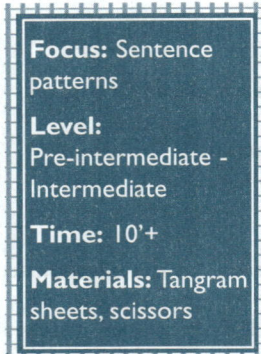

Tangram
(Groups)

Photocopiable material: p. 191

Focus: Sentence patterns

Level: Pre-intermediate - Intermediate

Time: 10'+

Materials: Tangram sheets, scissors

Procedure:

Students play in groups of three.
Decide on a sentence pattern that you want to practise.

e.g. Subject+Verb+Adverb or Subject +Verb+Object etc.
Write an example on the board.
e.g. She has worked here.
Ask students to give you words that replace has and here.
e.g. She never worked well.
Write another example on the board.
e.g. I won't wear hats.
Ask students to replace won't and hats.
e.g. I often wear red.

Give each group five copies of the tangram shape and scissors.
Groups write one sentence using the patterns they have practised on each tangram paper so they have five different sentences.
They start the sentence in the top left hand corner and continue in a clockwise direction.

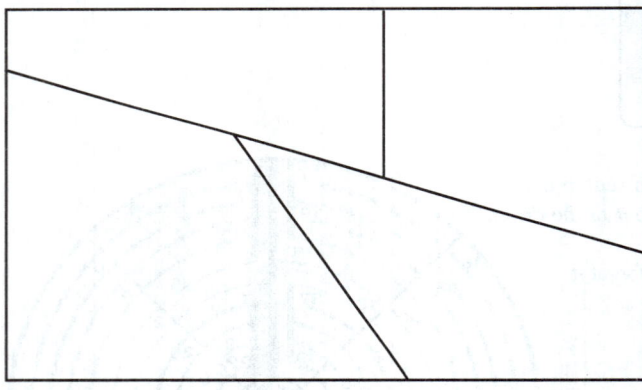 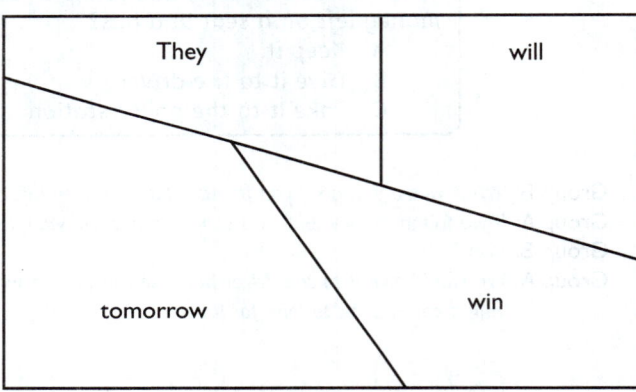

Students cut up the tangrams, shuffle the 20 pieces and swap them with another group.
The pieces are dealt out to the students in the group.
The students take it in turns to lay down a piece to complete the tangram.

e.g.   Student A: Puts They in the top left corner.
       Student B: Looks at their cards and picks will.
       Student C: Chooses win as the third word.
       Student A: Completes the tangram by putting down tomorrow.

The procedure is continued to build the next square.
The first square will be completed easily but in the following ones a student may not be able to go.
If a student cannot put a piece down, they can start a new tangram if they have a starting word.
The next student now has a choice of two tangrams to place a piece in.
Every sentence must make grammatical sense.
Any student can challenge the meaningfulness of a sentence and the student completing the square has to justify the meaning.
The winner is the first student to use all their pieces or, if nobody can put a piece down, the student with the least number of pieces in their hand.

Predictor
6 (Pairs)

Photocopiable material: p. 192

Focus: Any language area

Level: Pre-intermediate-Intermediate

Time: 10'+

Materials: paper, pencil

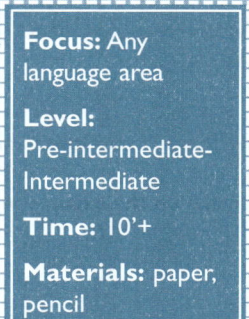

Procedure:

Students play in pairs.

Give students instructions on how to make a predictor from a square of paper.

Student A holds the predictor and asks student B to say a number. Student A opens and closes the predictor that many times to reveal four numbers in the centre. Student B chooses one of the four numbers and student A again opens and closes the predictor that many times.

Student B chooses one of the revealed numbers and that flap is opened to reveal a prediction.

Student A tells student B what is predicted on the inside flap and student B says whether they agree with the prediction or not and why.

e.g.　Student A: *Tell me a number.*
　　　Student B: *6*
　　　Student A: (opens - closes predictor 6 times to reveal numbers in the centre) *Choose a number.*
　　　Student B: *3*
　　　Student A: (opens and closes predictor 3 times) *Choose another number.*
　　　Student B: *8*
　　　Student A: (opens flap 8) *You will live in another country.*
　　　Student B: *I don't think I agree. I would like to visit many countries but I don't think I will live in another country.*

Student B gets a point for completing the task successfully and it is now student A's turn to play.

Other language areas that can be practised by writing different prompts on the predictor:

Prompt	Structure / Function	Language
Places	Present perfect/simple past	Have you been to …? When did you go?
Actions	Expressing preference	Would you like to fly a helicopter? Why (not)?
Food, activities	Likes/dislikes	Do you like …? Why (not)?
Situations (e.g. break a leg)	Second conditional	What would you do if you broke a leg?
Problems (e.g. a cough)	Giving advice (You should/ought to/If I were you/imperatives)	I've got a cough. If I were you, I'd take some medicine.
Times/dates/seasons	Simple past/Simple present	What did you do last weekend? I visited my grandparents.
Animals (e.g. elephant)	Qualities (is/has/do)	What do you know about elephants? An elephant is big and it has a long nose.
Objects (e.g. hair)	Verb+noun practice	What can you do with your hair? You wash hair, cut hair, brush hair.

Example with animals:

Each student makes a predictor and writes the names of different animals on the inside flaps.

e.g.　Student A: *Tell me a number.*
　　　Student B: *4*
　　　Student A: (opens and closes predictor 4 times) *Choose a number.*
　　　Student B: *5*
　　　Student A: (opens and closes predictor 5 times) *Choose another number.*
　　　Student B: *3*
　　　Student A: (opens flap 3) *Tell me three things about a parrot.*
　　　Student B: *It is usually colourful. It can talk. It has a strong beak.*

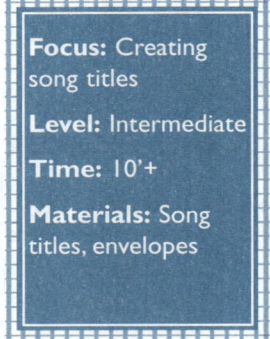

Our Song
(Groups)
7

Focus: Creating song titles	
Level: Intermediate	
Time: 10'+	
Materials: Song titles, envelopes	

Procedure:

Students play in groups of three.

Pick ten popular English song titles and write each word in a separate box on a grid.
Photocopy one page for each group. Cut out the word squares, shuffle them, put them in envelopes and hand them out to the groups.
Students lay the words out on a desk and try to find the original ten titles or make up their own song titles.
Each group has to try and use all the word squares.

Sample songs:

Cry	me	a	river				
All	the	things	she	said			
I'm	with	you					
Don't	know	why					
Wonder	where	you	are				
Times	like	these					
Sorry	seems	to	be	the	hardest	word	
Jenny	from	the	block				
Big	yellow	taxi					
A	thousand	miles					

The winner can be the group which is the first to use all the words, creates the longest meaningful title, makes up the most titles, or gets most of the original titles.

Sample titles:

Don't cry she said
The hardest block
A thousand yellow times

Where are you Jenny?
Be miles from the river
Seems to me like a taxi

Know the wonder
Why I'm with you
All these big sorry things

Sample longest sentence:
Seems to me a thousand miles from where I know you are Jenny.

Take 5
(Pairs)

Focus: Word order, meaning

Level: Intermediate

Time: 15'+

Materials: Cards, grid

Procedure:

Students play in pairs.
Each pair draws or is given two blank 5X5 grid cards. Students write five (five-word) sentences of identical structure on one grid card. They cut out the individual words, shuffle them and pass them to another pair. The students take twelve word cards each and turn them face up so they can see all their words.

e.g.

Pronoun	Time adverb	Verb	Preposition	Noun
I	never	speak	to	strangers
We	always	cook	on	Sundays
She	usually	goes	by	bus
He	sometimes	walks	to	work
They	rarely	arrive	on	time

e.g.

Pronoun	Time adverb	Verb	Preposition	Noun
	usually			
We	never	cook		

The remaining word card is placed in the correct cell, according to sentence structure, on the bottom row of the blank grid.
(e.g. If the remaining card is never, it goes at the bottom of column two.)

Students take it in turns to place one of their words on the grid.
Cells are filled from the bottom up, like building a wall.
Students can put a word down only above another word on the grid or in one of the bottom cells of the grid.
The word must be of the same type as the words in that column.

e.g. Student A doesn't have a time adverb and places **We** in the correct bottom cell.
Student B decides to put **usually** on top of never.
Student A places **cook** in the correct bottom cell.
Student B can now place a word in one of the two empty bottom cells or above **We**, **usually** or **cook**.

The student who places the last word to complete a sentence correctly, gets a point.

The winner is the student who has completed the most sentences that make sense.

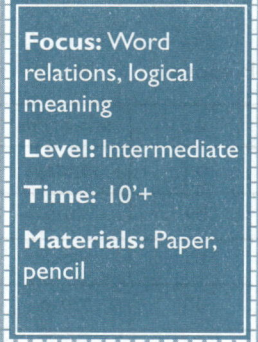

Take It Away
9 (Groups)

<table>
<tr><td>

Focus: Word relations, logical meaning

Level: Intermediate

Time: 10'+

Materials: Paper, pencil

</td></tr>
</table>

Procedure:

Divide the class into two groups.

Write a long sentence or short text on the board. Each group appoints a captain who comes to the front of the class. Groups take it in turns to tell their captain a word in the sentence to rub out. With the word removed, the sentence must still make sense although meaning and punctuation can change. If a group cannot remove a word, play goes to the other group.

e.g.
- *First, buy security locks for all doors and windows and a safety chain for the front door.*
  Group A: *Rub out front.*
- *First, buy security locks for all doors and windows and a safety chain for the door.*
  Group B: *Erase safety.*
- *First, buy security locks for all doors and windows and a chain for the door.*
  Group A: *Rub out security.*
- *First, buy locks for all doors and windows and a chain for the door.*

If the next four words deleted are *first, all, a* and *for*, the remaining text would be: *Buy locks for doors and windows and chain the door.*
The final sentence could be: *Buy locks, doors, windows and chain door.*
After each turn, the class, with the teacher, decides if the sentence still makes sense.
The winning team is the one that removes the last word before the sentence becomes meaningless.

Variation:

Students remove two words at a time.

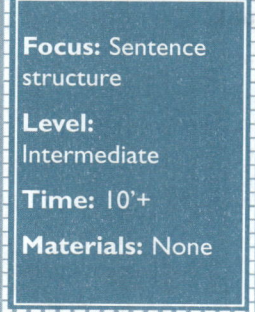

Mickey Makes Money
10 (Pairs)

<table>
<tr><td>

Focus: Sentence structure

Level: Intermediate

Time: 10'+

Materials: None

</td></tr>
</table>

Procedure:

Students play in pairs.

Students make up sentences a word at a time. Each word must begin with the same letter or sound. The first word must be a person's name.
Prepositions or articles can be added with the word but do not count as a separate turn.
Dictate a letter to the groups. Do not use the letters: J, K, Q, U, V, X, Y, Z.

e.g. Teacher: *M*
Student A: (says/writes) *Mickey*
Student B: *makes*
Student A: *money*
Student B: *in the morning*
Student A: *moving*
Student B: *millions*
Student A: *more*
Student B: *at midnight.*

Here's another example: *Sue sensibly suggested squirrels should start saving in the summer.*
If student A cannot think of a word to continue the sentence, the round ends there and student B gets a point. Student A then picks a new starting letter. The winner is the first student to win 10 points

Chains
(Groups)

Focus: Hypothetical events

Level: Intermediate-Upper-intermediate

Time: 10'+

Materials: Cards

Procedure:

Students play in groups of three.
Students write three statements on separate cards and pass them to another group.
Each group picks a card and starts a hypothetical chain, using the statement on the card.

e.g.

> Fall down – IF

Student A: *If I fall down, I might break my leg.*
Student B: *If I break my leg, I will go to hospital.*
Student C: *If I go to hospital, the doctor will put my leg in plaster.*
Student A: *If my leg is in plaster, it will heal.*
Student B: *If my leg heals, I will be able to play football.*
Student C: *If I play football, I might break my leg.*   etc

e.g.

> Be rich – IF

Student A: *If I were rich, I would buy a yacht.*
Student B: *If I bought a yacht, I would travel around the world.*
Student C: *If I travelled around the world, I would learn many things.*
Student A: *If I learnt many things, I could write a book.*
Student B: *If I wrote a book, it might be a best seller.*
Student C: *If the book were a best seller, I would become even richer.*

e.g.

> Go to Paris – IF

Student A: *If I hadn't gone to Paris, I wouldn't have met Pierre.*
Student B: *If I hadn't met Pierre, I wouldn't have learnt about art.*
Student C: *If I hadn't learnt about art, I wouldn't have become an artist.*
Student A: *If I hadn't become an artist, I wouldn't have become famous.*
Student B: *If I hadn't become famous, I wouldn't have made lots of money.*
Student C: *If I hadn't made lots of money, I wouldn't be living in Paris now.*

Variation:

Students add a word to a statement written on a card. Two words can be added only if one is simultaneously deleted. If two words are deleted, two must be added.

e.g.

> I like sweets.

Student A: *I like sweets.*
Student B: *I like sticky sweets*
Student C: *I do not like sweets.*
Student A: *I do not like sticky sweets.*
Student B: *I do not like very sticky sweets.*
Student C: *I like all very sticky chocolate sweets.*

The game stops when a student cannot add a new sentence to the chain. Students then start a new chain.

From Memory
(Groups)

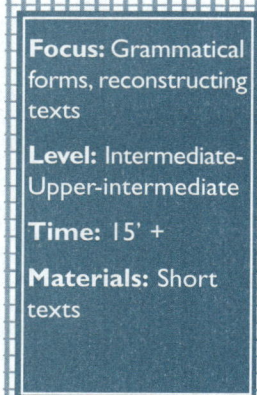

Focus: Grammatical forms, reconstructing texts

Level: Intermediate-Upper-intermediate

Time: 15' +

Materials: Short texts

Procedure:

Students play in groups of three.

Write or select a short paragraph which has examples of the grammatical area you wish to focus on. Draw a simple picture illustrating part of the story on the board. Students guess what it is. Elicit vocabulary students might not know.

Read the text once at normal speed. Then read the text again stopping briefly after each sentence so that students can write down key words. (Tell students not to try and write down every word.)

e.g.

I was looking forward to going to this island very much. I'd heard about it from friends who had been there and said it was wonderful. The first day I got there, I found the most amazing beach and was walking along it looking at the sea. I wasn't looking where I was going and suddenly I walked into the edge of a bamboo beach umbrella. I was knocked unconscious and must have been taken to the doctor's. I woke up there and discovered that the doctor had put ten stitches in my head. It was not a very good start to my holiday.

Students use the key words from each sentence and try to reconstruct the text.

In groups, students compare their texts and using this information write down a version that they feel is closest to the original.

Pick a student from one group to write their text on the board. Ask the other groups to read out their versions.

All the students now suggest changes to the text on the board to try and get it as close to the original as possible.

Finally, pass out copies of the original text or put it on an overhead projector and compare it with the reconstructed text. Groups get a point for every sentence in their text that is the same as the original. Reasons why certain structures were used can be elicited/given.

In reconstructing the text students are forced to think of which structure to use as they will not be able to do the task just from memory.

The group with the most points is the winner.

What will happen next?
(Groups)

Photocopiable material: p. 193

Focus: Sentence meaning, structure

Level: Intermediate

Time: 10' +

Materials: Cards, toothpicks

Procedure:

Divide the class into two groups.

Give each student five toothpicks. Photocopy sentence cards or have students write a sentence on a sheet of paper.

If the student picks a sentence card, they write that sentence at the top of a sheet of paper.

The sheets of paper are passed clockwise in the group. Each student has to add or delete a word in the sentence and write the new sentence under the original. Students then pass their paper to the next person.

e.g.

> What do you think
> will happen next?

Student A: What do you think will happen?
Student B: What do you really think will happen?
Student C: What do you really think will happen tomorrow?
Student D: What do you think will happen tomorrow?   etc

Sample Cards:

It was a dark and stormy night.	I saw him last night.	To be or not to be, that is the question.	We sat round the fire talking.
When in doubt, panic!	All that glitters is not gold.	Life is not a bowl of cherries.	Never say never.
The best food is cooked at home.	A man is known by the company he keeps.	People in glass houses should not throw stones.	When a man is tired of London, he is tired of life.

A word can only be added and deleted in the same position in the sentence once.

If a student cannot delete or add a word, they lose a toothpick.

The winners are the students who have the most toothpicks when their original sheet of paper returns to them.

4 Grammar

What's wrong?
14 (Pairs)

Photocopiable material: pp. 194-195

Focus: Error correction

Level: Intermediate

Time: 15' +

Materials: Cards

Procedure:

Students play in pairs.

Photocopy or prepare twenty cards with common student errors. On each card write one incorrect sentence and the corrected version (**bold**).

e.g.

> I work at one office.
> **I work in an office.**

> He lives in a big appartment.
> **He lives in a big apartment.**

Two pairs play against each other and are given a copy of the twenty cards.

The cards are placed face down on a desk between the pairs.

A student from one pair picks up a card and reads it out to the other pair. That pair must choose which sentence is the correct one. If they decide correctly, they win that card. If not, the card goes to the other team.

If the mistake is one of punctuation or spelling, when the card is read out the punctuation or spelling is also read.

The winner is the pair with the most cards.

Extension:

Students play in groups of three.

Each group is given a copy of the board and a set of error cards. The error cards are different for each group and do not have the correct version written on them. The cards are shuffled and placed in the centre of the board. Two groups play against each other. Groups take it in turns to pick up a card, decide what is wrong, and correct it orally. The card is then placed on the correct space on the board.

e.g.

> I am aplying for a credit card.

Correct answer: I am applying for a credit card.

EW = extra word
Sp = spelling
P = punctuation
WW = wrong word
MW = missing word
T = wrong verb tense
WO = word order
! = other mistakes

This card would be placed on the Sp space on the board.

The first group who places at least one card in each space wins.

WO	EW	Sp
T	Cards	P
MW	!	WW

Sample Cards:

> I am liking holidays.
> **I like taking holidays.**

> The English is difficult for me.
> **English is difficult for me.**

> How was it like?
> **What was it like?**

> She is a great city.
> **It is a great city.**

> Many mens do this.
> **Many men do this.**

> The people who they live there are friendly.
> **The people who live there are friendly.**

> I must to leave now.
> **I must leave now.**

> I lost the bus this morning.
> **I missed the bus this morning.**

> I always have to make the cooking.
> **I always have to do the cooking.**

> Where you went yesterday?
> **Where did you go yesterday?**

> It happened the same to me.
> **The same thing happened to me.**

> He has very much problems.
> **He has very many problems.**

Poetry In Motion
(Groups)

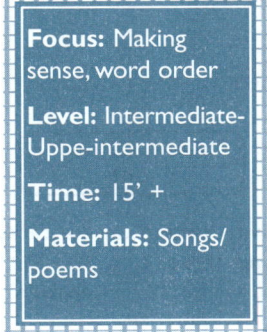

Focus: Making sense, word order

Level: Intermediate-Uppe-intermediate

Time: 15' +

Materials: Songs/poems

Procedure:

Students play in groups of three.

Find a suitable short poem or song verse, preferably one that is well known by students. (Adapt if necessary.)

e.g.	When	I get older, losing my	hair
	Many	years from	now.
	Will	you still be sending me lots of	treats,
	Birthday	greetings, boxes of	sweets?
	If	I stay out till quarter to	four
	Will	you lock the	door?
	Will	you still need	me?
	Will	you still feed	me?
	When	I'm	sixty-four?

(Adapted from The Beatles)

Remove all the words in each line between the first and last words. Give each group a copy of the verse with only the first and last words of each line and the number of missing words in brackets.

e.g.

When .... hair (5)	Will .... door? (3)
Many .... now. (2)	Will .... me? (3)
Will .... treats, (7)	Will .... me? (3)
Birthday .... sweets? (3)	When .... sixty-four? (1)
If .... four (6)	

Dictate the missing words in random order or give students the words on a piece of paper:

get	older	I	feed	years	lots	out	you	still	you	I	of	be	me
of	greetings	still	boxes	stay	quarter	to	losing	lock	you	sending	still	the
till	need	you	I'm	my	from	me						

Students try to complete the poem/song by putting the words in the correct place and order.

When all groups have completed their verse, or after a time limit, read out the original verse.

Students compare each line of their version with the corresponding line in the original and get one point for each word which is the same.

e.g. Original: When I get older, losing my hair
       Group A: When I don't have any more hair = 1 point
       Group B: When I have lost all my hair = 2 points

The winner is the pair with the most points.

Variation:

Students get the first and last words of each line and the number of words missing from each line.

In groups, students write their own version using the number of words indicated for each line.

Groups read out their version of the poem/song. After all the poems/songs have been read out, the class votes on the best one.

Just do it!
(Groups)

Photocopiable material: p. 196

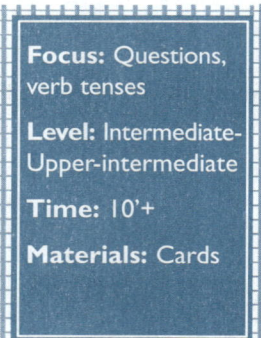

Focus: Questions, verb tenses

Level: Intermediate-Upper-intermediate

Time: 10'+

Materials: Cards

Procedure:

Students play in groups of three.
Photocopy or prepare and give each group cards with various activities on them.

e.g
live alone | go on holiday alone | give away your money | live in another country

Student A picks up a card and asks student B a question based on the activity written on the card. Student B replies and student A asks *Why?/Why not?*. Student B must answer three *Why?/Why not?* questions to get a point. (The responses must have a reason why and not just a *'because, I do'* answer.)

e.g. Student A: *Would you ever live alone?*
Student B: *Yes/No.*
Student A: *Why?/Why not?*
Student B: *I would live alone because I would like to have my friends over whenever I wanted.*
Student A: *Why would you want your friends over whenever you wanted?*
Student B: *I would want them over because I like their company.*
Student A: *Why do you like their company?*
Student B: *I like their company because they are fun.*

It is now student B's turn to pick up a card and ask student C a question. The winner is the student with the most points after each student has answered three cards.

Different language areas: Present perfect: Have you ever gone camping? Past simple: You stayed up all night. Why? Going to: You painted your room black. Why?

What's your story?
(Groups)

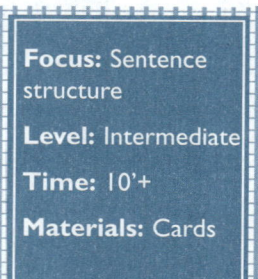

Focus: Sentence structure

Level: Intermediate

Time: 10'+

Materials: Cards

Procedure:

Students play in groups of three.
Write a one sentence story of fixed length and structure on the board. Students individually compose three sentences, writing each section on separate cards based on the model.
e.g.

One day	an old man	was walking	down the road	when	his wife	called him. [model]
Last week	a brown dog	was sleeping	in my yard	and	our cat	scared it.
Yesterday	my little sister	was going	to the park	but	my mum	stopped her.

The cards are collected, shuffled and dealt to the group.
Students attempt to be the first to get rid of their cards by taking turns to put one card at a time on the table to create a story sentence.
e.g.   Student A: One day
       Student B: a brown dog
       Student C: was going...   etc.
The sentences may not be the same as the originals, but anything that makes sense is acceptable.

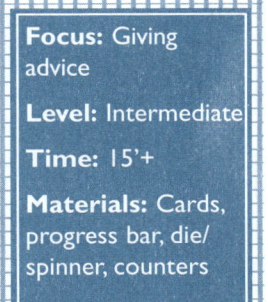

Help!
(Groups)

Photocopiable material: pp. 197-199

Focus: Giving advice

Level: Intermediate

Time: 15'+

Materials: Cards, progress bar, die/spinner, counters

Procedure:

Students play in groups of three.
Review/Elicit language for giving advice from students. Write a list on the board.

e.g. You should...   If I were you...   Why don't you...   How about...   It might be a good idea to...
You could...   Why not ...   You'd better...   You ought to...   Have you thought of...

Explain to students that they will be going on a cross-country cycling tour and that they will encounter certain problems along the way.
Photocopy or prepare and give each group a set of problem and advice cards, a progress bar, counters and die/spinner. There should be more advice cards than problem cards.

Each student puts their counter on the central square (0) of the progress bar:

-10	-9	-8	-7	-6	-5	-4	-3	-2	-1	0	1	2	3	4	5	6	7	8	9	10

Students put the two piles of cards face down under the bar.
Student A picks up a problem card and reads it out. Students B and C pick up an advice card and using language from the board, give advice to student A.
The advice may not always fit the situation but students must try to give reasons why their advice would be appropriate.
Student A chooses the advice they think is the best.

e.g.   Student A: *I have a flat tyre.*
Student B: *If I were you, I would take the bus to the nearest garage.*
Student C: *Why not try finding a mechanic. He could fix your flat tyre.*

Student A chooses student B's advice and must now face the consequences of taking that advice. Student B rolls/spins to advance student A's counter. Student B also moves their counter the same number of spaces.
e.g.
Roll/spin shows 1 or 2, student A moves back one space.
Roll/spin shows 3 or 4, student A moves forward one space.
Roll/spin shows 5 or 6, student A moves forward two spaces.

Used problem and advice cards are placed at the bottom of the piles. It is now student B's turn to pick a problem card. The student who reaches the end of the progress bar first, wins.

Sample Problem Cards:

Have a flat tyre.	Lose map.	Lose pedal.	Tent blows away.

Sample Advice Cards:

Find a mechanic.	Stop and camp.	Take the bus.	Call a doctor.

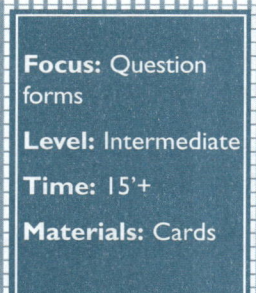

What's up?
(Groups)

Photocopiable material: p. 200

Focus: Question forms

Level: Intermediate

Time: 15'+

Materials: Cards

Procedure:

Divide the class into two groups.
Photocopy or have students prepare sets of problem cards.
Each card defines:
what the problem is.
what caused it.
what action will be taken.

e.g.

> You have stomach ache.
> You ate some seafood that was off.
> You are going to go to bed.

Give each group a set of different problem cards.
A student from group A picks up a card, shows it to his group then, mimes the problem for group B.
Group B can ask 12 yes/no questions to find the problem, cause and action.

e.g.   Group B: *Are you in pain?*
      Group A: *Yes, I am.*
      Group B: *Do you have stomach ache?*
      Group A: *Yes, I do.*

Now that group B has guessed the problem, the student from group A mimes the cause.
      Group B: *Did you eat something bad?*
      Group A: *Yes, I did.*
      Group B: *Was it meat?*
      Group A: *No, it wasn't.*
      Group B: *Was it seafood?*
      Group A: *Yes, it was.*

The student from group A now mimes the problem and cause again, adding a mime for the action that will be taken.
      Group B: *Are you going to the doctor?*
      Group A: *No, I'm not.*
      Group B: *Are you going for a walk?*
      Group A: *No, I'm not.*   etc.

If group B find the three parts on the card they win that card.
The winner is the group that wins the most cards.

Sample Cards:

> You are afraid.
> There is an earthquake.
> You are going to hide under the table.

> You are cold.
> There is no heating in the house.
> You are going to go to bed.

> You can't get into your house.
> You have lost your keys.
> You go and stay at a friend's.

> You are hot.
> You are sunbathing on the beach.
> You are going to buy an ice cream.

> You can't sleep.
> You have an exam in the morning.
> You are going to listen to some music.

> Your eyes ache.
> You have been working on the computer too long.
> You are going to take a break.

And, So, But
(Groups)

Photocopiable material: pp. 201-203

Focus: Linking words

Level: Intermediate

Time: 15'+

Materials: Cards, board

Procedure:

Students play in groups of three.
Give each group a photocopy of the board and sets of triangle cards. On one set of cards prepare or have students write sentence prompts. The other three sets are marked with the conjunctions and, but, so or any other connecting words you wish to practise. e.g. however, therefore, then, etc.
The triangle cards may be colour coded.

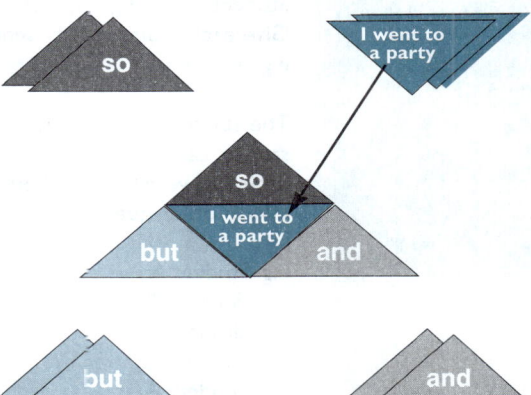

Student A picks up a sentence card, reads it to the group, places it in the centre triangle and adds one of the joining words. Student B continues the sentence in their own words and adds a second linking word. Student C does the same. Student A can now complete the sentence.

e.g.   Student A: *I went to a party and...*
Student B: *I met a girl but...*
Student C: *she wouldn't dance with me, so...*
Student A: *I left in a bad mood.*

When the sentence is completed, the cards are removed from the board and student B picks up a new sentence prompt card and starts a new game.

Sample Cards:

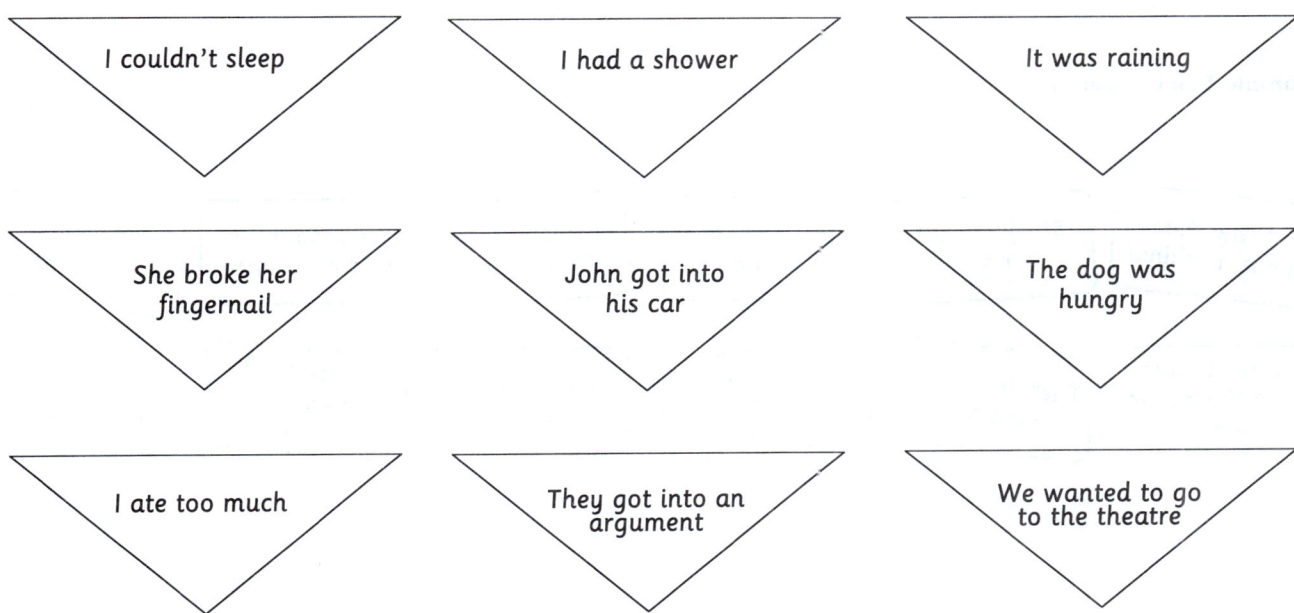

I couldn't sleep

I had a shower

It was raining

She broke her fingernail

John got into his car

The dog was hungry

I ate too much

They got into an argument

We wanted to go to the theatre

Questions, Questions
21   (Groups)

Photocopiable material: pp. 204-205

Focus: Question forms, getting information

Level: Intermediate

Time: 10'+

Materials: Cards

Procedure:

Students play in groups of three.
Give each group twenty sentence starter cards and eighteen question prompt cards.
e.g. how, when, where, why, who, what - 3 of each

The starter cards and question cards are placed face down in two separate piles. Student A picks up a starter card and reads out the situation. Student B picks up a question card and forms a question beginning with the word on the card. Student A replies and Student C then picks up a question card and asks another question.

e.g. Student A: *I've crashed it.*
       Student B: *Where did it happen?*
       Student A: *It happened at the corner of Rose and Maple Streets.*
       Student C: *When did it happen?*
       Student A: *It happened yesterday.*

Students continue to ask and answer questions until a question word appears which has already been used. Student B now picks up a different starter card and the game continues.

Question Cards [3 of each]

| How? | When? | Where? | Why? | Who? | What? |

Sample Starter Cards:

| I saw this amazing thing! | She just said no. | Then it all went wrong. | We were feeling pretty good. | We thought we had no chance. | I had just missed her. |

| It must have been the wrong day. | Then the lights went out. | It was absolutely awful! | I'll never do that again! | It was much too early for that. | It was a dream come true. |

Verb Draughts
(Pairs)

22

Photocopiable material: p. 206

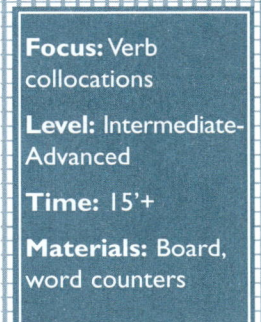

Focus: Verb collocations

Level: Intermediate-Advanced

Time: 15'+

Materials: Board, word counters

Procedure:

Students play in pairs.

Give each pair a photocopy of the board. Students prepare word counters (12 grey, 12 white) by writing a verb on each of the counters. The verbs can be the same for both grey and white players.

e.g.

| MAKE | HAVE | GIVE | WEAR | GET | HIT |
| DO | TAKE | PUT | LOSE | BREAK | CATCH |

The rules for playing the game are the same as for draughts (checkers).

Students put their counters on the first three lines nearest them, but only on the black squares so the grey and white counters face each other. Students take turns to move one counter at a time. Counters can only move forward diagonally, one space at a time, to another black ssquare.

When a counter is moved, the player must use the verb written on it with a collocating noun to make a sentence.

e.g. MAKE - I made a mistake.

If the same counter is moved again later in the game, the collocating noun must be different.

If the collocation is incorrect the student cannot move the counter.   e.g. I made my homework.

The aim is to take your opponent's pieces by jumping over them and removing them from the board.

In order to take an opponent's counter, the student must make a sentence using the verb on the opponent's counter as well as their own counter.

A student can take more than one counter at a time if the opponents counters are in the right postion.

If a student reaches a square on their opponent's back line, that piece becomes a king and another counter of the same colour is placed on top of it. This counter can now be moved using any of the verbs on the counters.

The king can move backwards as well as forwards diagonally.

The winner is the one who captures all of their opponent's pieces.

5 Pronunciaton

Give me a call!
1 (Groups)

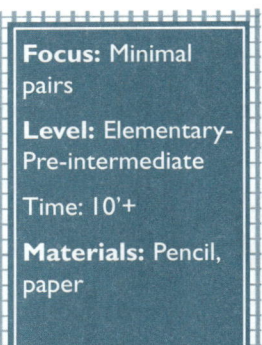

Focus: Minimal pairs

Level: Elementary-Pre-intermediate

Time: 10'+

Materials: Pencil, paper

Procedure:

Students play in groups of three.
Write a set of problematic or confusing minimal pairs on the board, each one corresponding to a number from 0 – 9.
Start by reading a word to the class. Students say what number the word corresponds to. Do this with all the words.

e.g   Teacher: *chip*
         Students: *two*
         Teacher: *sink*
         Students: *five*

0	shop	1	chop
2	chip	3	cheap
4	sing	5	sink
6	think	7	thing
8	but	9	bat

Explain to the class that you will read out a telephone number using the word code, and that you will say each word twice. Read out the telephone number in code by saying each word twice. Students listen to the words and write down the corresponding numbers.

e.g.   Teacher: *Sing,sing. Sink, sink. Cheap, cheap. Chip, chip. Think, think. Thing, thing. Bat, bat.*
         Students: *4532679*

In groups of three, students take it in turns to use the code to dictate made-up phone numbers to their group. The other students in the group write down the numbers corresponding to the words they hear. Then they check their answers with the speaker at the end.
Students who write down the correct telephone number get a point. The winner is the student with the most points.
You can play the game again with different minimal pairs.

e.g.
Hard – had	bay – buy	cot – got	her – hair	fin – thin
Rise – rice	run – one	gong – gone	fry – fly	ten – den

Alternative:

Two words are read out loud. Students add the corresponding numbers and say what the sum is using the code words.

e.g   Student A: *thing and sink*
         Students add the numbers 7 and 5 together to get 12
         Student B: *chop and chip* (this would represent the numbers one and two)

I think I sink...

Sound Bingo
(Class)

2

☞ **Pointer:**

Bingo games are an enjoyable way to practise a variety of language, including sounds, opposites, synonyms and irregular verbs.

Focus: Minimal pairs

Level: Elementary

Time: 10'+

Materials: Word list, pencil, paper

Procedure:

Give each student a sheet of paper with 20 words on it. In this case 10 minimal pairs. Each student chooses any ten words and circles these in pen.

e.g.

| (hit) | heat | fit | (feet) | (hang) | hung | deep | (dip) | trip | (drip) |
| (her) | hair | (hope) | hop | hurt | (heart) | (bed) | bead | (gold) | cold |

Read out any ten words at random, making sure they are not in the same order as on the sheet of paper. Keep a note of which words you have called out.

If a student has circled any of the words that are read out, they put a line through that word.

When a student thinks they have heard and crossed out the ten words they circled, they call out: *'Bingo!'*

Check the student's card to make sure they crossed off the words you said.

Students then play the game in groups. One student is the caller, and the students have a new list of words to circle.

Alternative:

Write on the board or give the students a list of 25 words you want them to practise. Give each student a blank bingo card and have the students fill in each cell of the grid (with one word only) until the card is full. Students may put the words wherever they like on the grid.

e.g.   **Student A's card:**

(heart)	deep	trip	hit	bead
heat	(drip)	dip	hope	sheep
cold	hop	(her)	fit	think
bead	hung	hair	(hurt)	cheap
bed	feet	hang	gold	(thing)

Call out words from the list at random.

Students use a pencil to circle the words they hear.

When a student has circled all the words in a line (across, down or diagonally) on their card they connect them with a line and call out *'Bingo!'*.

Check the card to see whether the words the student crossed off are the words you called out.

If the correct words are circled, the student gets a point. If not, the student rubs out any mistakes they have made.

The game continues until all the words have been called out.

The winner is the student with the most points at the end.

Students can then play the game in groups with one student in each group calling out the words.

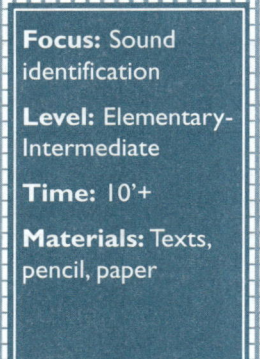

How many times do you hear ...?
3 (Class)

Focus: Sound identification

Level: Elementary-Intermediate

Time: 10'+

Materials: Texts, pencil, paper

Procedure:

Explain to the class that you will be reading a short text focusing on particular sounds/combinations. Tell the students what sound to listen for, giving examples of other words which have the same sound. e.g. for the vowel sound /i/ - r**ea**d, n**ee**d, l**ea**n, m**ea**t.

Read the text at normal speed to the class.
Students put a tick on a piece of paper every time they think they hear the sound.
Students add up the ticks. Check to see which students have the correct number.

e.g. Students are asked to focus on the vowel sound they hear in the word read - /i/.

Students listen and tick. (four instances are heard)
The same text could be used to focus on other sounds.
e.g. /**sh**/. (three instances are heard)

> In some seasons you see, shepherds keep the silly sheep inside a shed.

Texts can be easily made up or found in poetry collections.
e.g. Students could be asked to focus on **b** and **p** consonants:

> I picked a big bunch of pink pansies to present to beautiful big Bertha, the bald princess.

Ask students these questions:
*How many times do you hear the **P** sound?*   Answer: 5
*How many times do you hear the **B** sound?*   Answer: 6

Students get one point for every correct sound they hear. The winner is the student with the most points after each round.

Extension:

Ask the class for five words containing a sound you want them to practise. e.g. /ch/ as in **ch**ip. Write the words on the board.
e.g.   **ch**eap   **ch**in   **ch**air   whi**ch**   **ch**icken

Ask the class for another five words containing a contrasting sound. e.g. /sh/ as in **sh**ip and write these on the board also.
e.g.   wa**sh**   **sh**oe   wi**sh**   **sh**ampoo   fi**sh**

In pairs, students write a sentence using two words from each of the lists on the board.
e.g. Wa**sh** the **ch**icken with **ch**eap **sh**ampoo.
      I wi**sh** **ch**icken was as **ch**eap as fi**sh**.

Pairs take it in turns to read their sentences to the class. The other pairs can win a point if they can substitute one of the /sh/ or /ch/ words with a new /sh/ or /ch/ word which is not on the board. Set a time limit of 15 seconds.
As soon as a pair has an answer, they read the whole sentence with their new word to the class.

e.g. Wash the chicken with *shiny* shampoo.
      I wish chicken was as cheap as *chips*.

Pairs continue to replace /sh/ or /ch/ words if they can, winning a point each time.
If nobody can replace any of the words in the original sentence, the pair who wrote the sentence wins a point.
The next pair then read their sentence.
The winners are the pair with the most points when all the written sentences have been read out and changed where possible.

Tongue Twisters
4 (Groups)

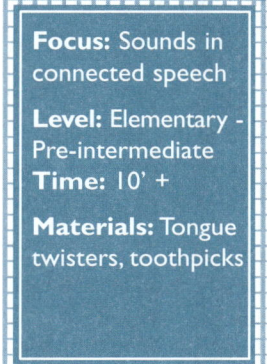

Focus: Sounds in connected speech

Level: Elementary - Pre-intermediate
Time: 10' +

Materials: Tongue twisters, toothpicks

☞ **Pointer:**

Tongue twisters focus on particular sounds and are difficult even for native speakers to say, so they are meant for fun.

Procedure:

Students play in groups of three.
Use the following tongue twisters or others you may know and read them out loud to the class. Have the students repeat them after you.

e.g. *Swan, swim over the sea. Swim, swan, swim! Swan, swim back again. Well swum, swan!*
Betty Botter had some batter.
She sells seashells on the seashore.
Put a better bit of butter on your bread.
Sister Suzy's sewing shirts for soldiers.
Red lorry, yellow lorry.
Busy buzzing bumblebees.
Round the rugged rocks the ragged rascal ran.
Peter Piper picked a peck of pickled peppers.
How much wood would a woodchuck chuck, if a woodchuck could chuck wood?

Students individually make up their own 3 word tongue twisters, each word having the same sound in it.

e.g. *Bring baby's breakfast*
Cars come quickly
Sing something simple
Live loving life
Hamsters have hair

Give each student five toothpicks.
Student A reads out their tongue twister to the group and the other students repeat it once.
Going around the group, each student now repeats the tongue twister twice, then three times as quickly as they can.
Each time a student stumbles over or mispronounces the tongue twister, they lose a toothpick and place it in the centre of the table.
In the next round, they can regain the lost toothpick if they say the tongue twister correctly.
Now, it is student B's turn to read out their tongue twister.

The winner is the student with the most toothpicks after all the tongue twisters have been read out.

Whispering Messages
(Groups)

Photocopiable material: p. 207

Give peace a chance.

Give fish a dance?

Focus: Listening and remembering
Level: Elementary-Intermediate
Time: 10'+
Materials: Cards

Procedure:

Students sit in a horseshoe shape.

If you have more than ten students, form two groups.

Have each student write four related words or a phrase on a card.

The cards are numbered, shuffled and placed next to the first student at one end of the horseshoe.

Student A, at the start of the horseshoe, picks up a card, reads it silently, puts the card face down next to the pile, and whispers the words on the card to student B.

Student B then turns and whispers what they think they heard to student C.

This goes on around the group until the last student in the group receives the message.

The last student at the other end of the horseshoe, writes down the message they hear on a blank card and places it face down next to them.

As soon as student B has passed the message to student C, student A picks up another card and repeats the procedure and sends another message into the chain until all the messages are circulating around the horseshoe.

When the student at the end of the horseshoe has written down the last message, student A reads out the first message card and the last student reads out their received version of the message to see how close it is to the original.

When there are two or more groups playing, the group that gets the message correct wins a point. The winner is the group with the most points.

Words – Four related words on each card.

e.g. Food:

1 banana, lamb, vegetable, milk	2 chicken, apple, rice, cornflakes	3 cabbage, bread, cake, salt

Phrases – Common conversational phrases up to 7 words.

e.g.

1 Have you got the time?	2 Nice day today, isn't it?	3 Do you come here often?

Quotes – Cliches and proverbs.

e.g.

1 Give peace a chance.	2 To be or not to be.	3 You can't take it with you.

Sample Cards: for cliches and proverbs

The best is yet to come.	Too many cooks spoil the broth.	Time is money.
As old as the hills.	A stitch in time saves nine.	Every cloud has a silver lining.
Better to be happy than rich.	Laugh and the world laughs with you.	Once bitten twice shy.

Extension:

With advanced students, give message cards to the students at both ends of the horseshoe to send along the chain at the same time.

Rhyming Couplets
6 (Pairs)

Photocopiable material: p. 208

> **Focus:** Writing rhyming poems
>
> **Level:** Elementary-Intermediate
>
> **Time:** 10'+
>
> **Materials:** Cards, pencil, paper

Procedure:

Students play in pairs.
Photocopy or prepare different rhyming word cards and give each pair a set.
At elementary level, pairs make up 2 line rhyming couplets.
The rhyming words on the card must be at the end of the lines.

e.g. **Card:** | hat/cat |

Pair A: *I have a cat,*
He has a hat.

At higher levels, pairs first brainstorm any other words they know which rhyme with the given words, then write a four line rhyming poem. If getting four lines to rhyme proves difficult, students can write the first two lines with the same rhyme and the second two with a different rhyme.

e.g. **Card:** | higher/choir |

Pair A: *A singer in the **choir**,*
*Tried to sing much **higher**,*
*He tripped upon a **wire**,*
*And now he is a **crier**.*

Pair B: *A singer in the **choir**,*
*Tried to sing much **higher**,*
*He thought it such a **blow**,*
*That his voice was very **low**.*

Pairs take it in turns to read out their poems to the class who votes on the best one.

Alternative:

Give each pair a different opening line. Pairs copy their line on a piece of paper and write a second line making sure the last word rhymes with the last word of the first line. Pairs pass their paper to the their right. The pair that receives the paper adds another rhyming line and passes it to the next pair. The game stops when a pair cannot add a rhyming line. Pairs read out the poems to the class who votes on the best one.

e.g. Pair A: *A monkey in the **zoo**,*
*Looked very much like **you**,*
Pair B: *I went to have a **view**,*
Pair C: *And found that it was **true**.*

> **Sample lines:**
>
> The thing I want to **say**,   The man up in the **moon**,
> A Martian came to **town**,   A person who was **sad**,
> I tried to sing a **song**,   I do not like to **wait**,
> A girl whose name was **Polly**,   I had a lot to **eat**,

Sample Cards:

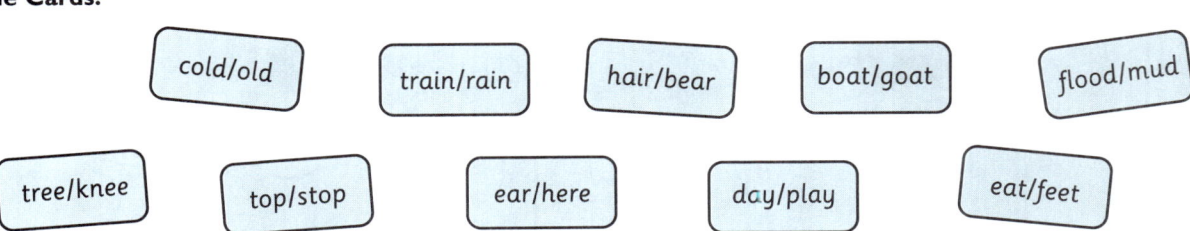

cold/old   train/rain   hair/bear   boat/goat   flood/mud

tree/knee   top/stop   ear/here   day/play   eat/feet

Number one kicked the ball

7 (Class)

> ☞ **Pointer:**
>
> If you have more than ten students, then two students can share the same number.

Focus: Sentence stress, rhythm

Level: Elementary-Pre-intermediate

Time: 10+

Materials: Cards

Procedure:

Students sit or stand in a circle.

Prepare a set of number cards from 1-10. Pick one number and write it in red.

Give each student a card and tell them not to show their number to anyone else. Students memorise the number and put the card face down.

Tell the class that the person who has the number written in red is the 'guilty one'.

The class will try and guess the guilty person at the end of the round.

Start a clapping rhythm in 4/4 time: 1,2,3,4. Students all clap together.

Teach the students the chant by saying each line and getting the class to repeat it. Then start off the game by saying the first line and the students continue it. Claps come on the syllables in bold.

e.g.   Teacher: *Number **one** kicked the **ball** and **broke** the **glass.***
Class: *Was it **you** number **one**?*
Student A: *Who **me**?*
Class: *Yes, **you**!*
Student A: *Not **me**!*
Class: *Then **who**?*
Student A: *Number **two** kicked the **ball** and **broke** the **glass.***
Class: *Was it **you** number **two**?*
Student B: *Who **me**?*
Class: *Yes, **you**!*
Student B: *Not **me**!*
Class: *Then **who**?*
Student B: *Number **three** kicked ...* etc.

At the end of the round, all students, including the one with the red card, write down who they think the guilty one is. Students who guess correctly get a point. Ask some of the students who guessed correctly to tell you why they think that person is the guilty one.

The start-off sentence can be whatever accusation you want to make up:

e.g.   *Number one:*   *took the apple from the teacher's desk.*
kissed the baby and made it cry.
broke the window and had to pay.
lost the keys and couldn't get in.

Nonsense poems
(Pairs)

☞ **Pointer:**

Creating nonsense words and in this way exploring the possibilities of language is natural to all cultures. In this type of activity, students don't have to think about the meaning of the word and can focus on the sounds and how they are spelled.

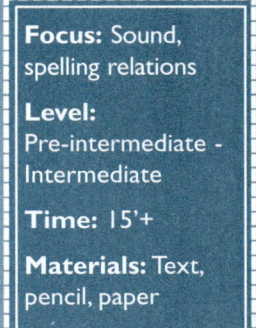

Focus: Sound, spelling relations

Level: Pre-intermediate - Intermediate

Time: 15'+

Materials: Text, pencil, paper

Procedure:

Students play in pairs.
Make up a poem with nonsense words for sound/spelling relations.
First, read out the poem as a whole. Then, read line by line as a dictation and students write down what they hear.
Tell students how many nonsense words there are. In this example there are nine.

e.g. *Jibber jabber said the monkey,*
Sluther sheever went the snail,
Whocker poozer called the whoopee,
Glatch that monkey's fibbly tail!

In pairs, students compare their work and agree together on the spelling of the nonsense words.
Pairs swap papers.
Write the poem on the board and have students mark the paper in front of them.
Each nonsense word spelled as in the original gets a point.
The pair with the most points wins.

It is also possible to make up a whole poem of 100% nonsense words for sound/spelling relations.

e.g. *Mordor, meerder, mider, moo,*
Chundor, cheeder, chider, choo,
Peelag, boolick, follen, mun,
Teewag, joolick, bollen, wun.

Extension:

Pairs write their own four-line nonsense poems and take it in turns to read them to the class.

Sounds Right
(Groups)

Photocopiable material: pp. 225-228

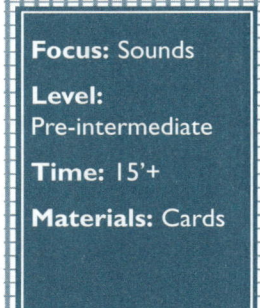

Focus: Sounds

Level: Pre-intermediate

Time: 15'+

Materials: Cards

Procedure:

Students play in groups of three.
Choose four English phonological sounds that your students have difficulty with.
Allocate each sound a symbol.

e.g.
🌐 = sh / [as in ship]
🦢 = ch [as in chip]
🍎 = j [as in jump]
🐦 = h [as in help]

On separate cards, write ten words for each category so you have forty different word cards.
Each symbol has 10 cards numbered 1 to 10.

e.g.

🌐 1	🦢 7	🍎 9	🐦 4
Shop	Chin	Joy	Hand

Shuffle and give each group a set of 40 cards. Each student gets *seven* cards and the remaining cards are placed face down in the centre of the desk. The top card is turned over and placed next to the pile.
Students take it in turns to put down a card on top of the upturned card on the table. A student can put a card down only if it has the *same number* as the one down, or if it has the *same symbol* with one number higher or lower than the card down. If a student does not have such a card they pick up a card from the pile. If they can put it down, they do so. If they can't put it down, they pick any of their cards and put it at the bottom of the pile. Each time a student puts down a card, they must say the word on that card. The winner is the first one to put down all seven cards.

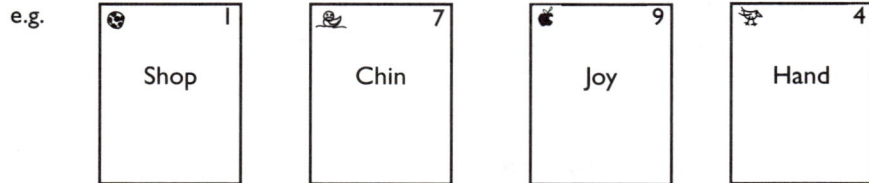

e.g. **Card down:**

🐦 4
Hand

→ Student A: *Shop*

🌐 4
Shop

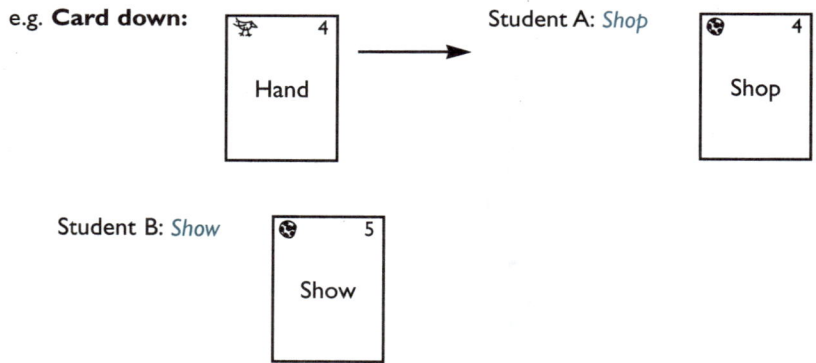

Student B: *Show*

🌐 5
Show

Student C: (Does not have a card to put down, so picks one up from the face down pile and puts one of their cards at the bottom of the pile.) *Hall*

🐦 6
Hall

Chants
10 (Class)

Focus: Sentence stress, rhythm

Level: Pre-intermediate-Intermediate

Time: 10'+

Materials: Rhymes

☞ **Pointer:**

Chants incorporate and exemplify the stress patterns in natural English speech in a memorable way.

Procedure:

Find or make up, short 4 line verses with regular stress patterns of 4 beats to each line. (It sounds better if two of the lines rhyme.)
In the following rhyme the stressed syllables are in bold and the final beat of lines 2 and 4 are silent.

e.g.   Mary had a little lamb,
     Its fleece was white as snow.
     And everywhere that Mary went,
     The lamb was sure to go.

When teaching the chant to the class, start up a clapping rhythm (softly 1,2,3,4). While clapping, say the first line, then get the class to repeat. Go through the chant line by line, having the students repeat after you. Put the first two lines together, then the second two and finally all four lines. [X= clap]

e.g.

     X   X   X   X
Get up at half past seven,
      X   X   X   X
Leave home at ten past eight.
       X   X   X   X
The school bell rings at twenty to nine,
   X   X   X   X
I hope I won't be late.

Each chant can focus on a particular structure, function or lexical field.
e.g.

For present perfect:
   I've never been to Russia.
   I've never been to France.
   I'd love to go to Egypt,
   If I ever get the chance.

For wish + past:
   I wish I were a little bird.
   I wish I had two wings.
   I wish I were a nightingale,
   I like the way it sings.

For telling the time:
   Get up at half past seven,
   Leave home at ten past eight.
   The school bell rings at twenty to nine,
   I hope I won't be late.

Extension:

Students play in pairs. Give pairs the first line of a verse which uses language you wish to practise. Pairs write the next three lines and then perform the chant for the class. The class votes for the best one.
Various poems such as nursery rhymes, cumulative rhymes, and limericks.with a strong rhythm also reinforce the natural patterns of English.
e.g.   Jack and Jill went up the hill to fetch a pail of water,
     Jack fell down and broke his crown and Jill came tumbling after.

e.g.   There was a little girl and she had a little curl
     Right in the middle of her forehead.
     When she was good she was very very good
     But when she was bad she was horrid.

Variation:

Instead of saying the chants, they could be sung as jogging chants, where the leader sings a line and the rest repeat.

Sound & Spelling
(Pairs)

11

Photocopiable material: p. 209

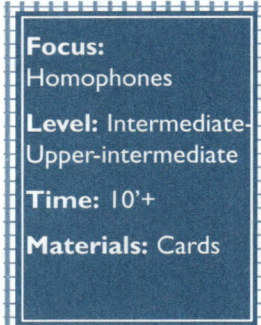

Focus: Homophones

Level: Intermediate-Upper-intermediate

Time: 10'+

Materials: Cards

Procedure:

Students play in pairs.

Give each pair a pile of cards. Each card has two words on it. Both words sound the same but have a different spelling and meaning.

Student A picks up a card and makes up and says a sentence using one of the words.

Student B decides **which** word in the sentence they heard was one of the two words on the card and spells it out loud.

If student B guesses correctly they try to make a sentence themselves with the **other** word on the card (which they know sounds the same). If student B does all this correctly, they keep that card.

e.g. **Card:** sea/see

Student A: *The sea has waves when it is windy.*
Student B: *S-E-A.*
Student A: *Correct.*
Student B: *I see what you mean.*

Student B then picks up a card and the game continues.
The winner is the one with the most cards when the card pile is finished.

Sample cards:

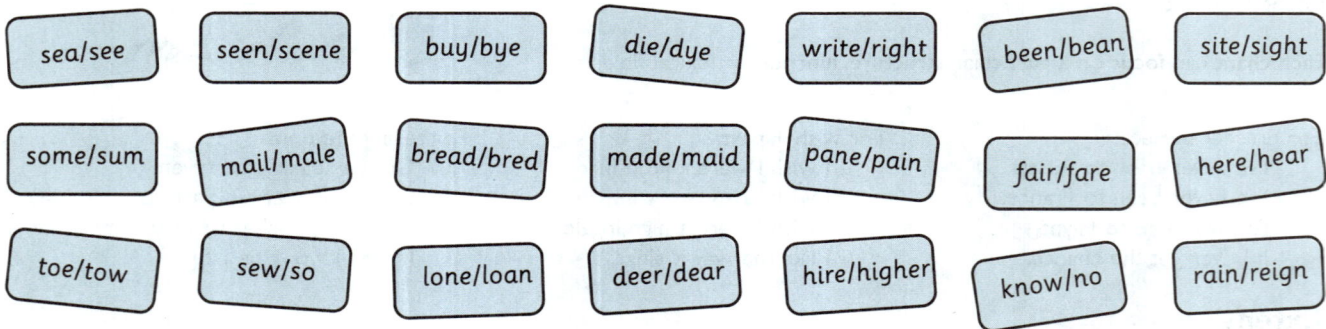

sea/see   seen/scene   buy/bye   die/dye   write/right   been/bean   site/sight

some/sum   mail/male   bread/bred   made/maid   pane/pain   fair/fare   here/hear

toe/tow   sew/so   lone/loan   deer/dear   hire/higher   know/no   rain/reign

Extension:

Pairs pick up a card and write a sentence using both words.

e.g. *Can you see the sea?*
      Have you seen that scene?
      This is the right way to write.

The pair with the shortest meaningful sentence wins.

Alternative:

Pairs have a time limit of 2 minutes in which to write as many meaningful sentences as they can from the cards they pick up.
The pair who writes the most sentences wins.

Vowel Shift
(Groups)

Photocopiable material: pp. 210, 229-231

Focus: Sound and meaning changes

Level: Intermediate

Time: 15'+

Materials: Cards, vowel tiles

Procedure:

Students play in groups of three.
Prepare 20 vowel tiles - A, E, I, O, and U - four copies of each vowel, and put them in a bag or envelope.

Give each student six blank word cards. Students look through a variety of texts from their coursebook and find 4 or 5 letter words from which they can remove a vowel to make a new word. Students write each of the new words on a separate card.

e.g. **BEAT** ⟶ | BAT | or | BET |

Collect and mix up the cards. Give each group an equal number of the word cards, which they place in a pile, face down. Give each group 10 blank cards or blank letter tiles.

Pick ten vowel cards from the bag or envelope and read them to the class. The students write down each vowel as you say it on a separate blank card/tile and place all the cards/tiles face up on the table next to the word card pile.

Student A picks up a word card from the pile, turns it over so everyone can see it, and uses the word in a sentence to show the meaning. Student B uses one of the vowel cards/tiles to make a new word from the one down, puts it in a sentence and if successful, keeps the cards used. Student C now picks up a word card from the pile and the game continues. If a student cannot use a vowel card to make a new word, play passes to the next student.

When all the cards have been used or no one can use the remaining vowel cards/tiles with a word card, the student with the most cards wins.

e.g.

Student A:	BET	*I bet you don't know what happened to Peter.*
Student B:	A	*I beat my cousin at tennis.*
Student C:	MAN	*Man is the cleverest animal.*
Student A:	I	*The main entrance is on the south side of the building.*

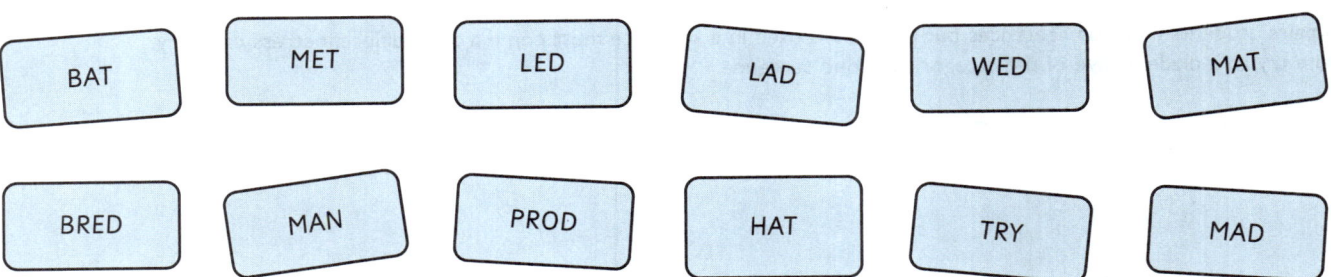

Sample Cards:

| BAT | MET | LED | LAD | WED | MAT |

| BRED | MAN | PROD | HAT | TRY | MAD |

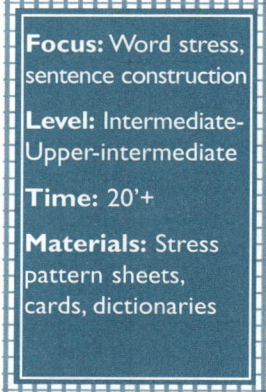

Word Patterns
(Pairs)

Photocopiable material: p. 211

Focus: Word stress, sentence construction

Level: Intermediate-Upper-intermediate

Time: 20'+

Materials: Stress pattern sheets, cards, dictionaries

Procedure:

Students play in pairs.
Photocopy the stress pattern sheet and give each pair a copy or get them to copy the patterns from the board and make their own. Give each pair a set of blank cards.
Students search various texts to find multi-syllable words.
Each pair should find at least three words to fit under each stress pattern.
Students may use the three blank columns on their sheet with words of other stress patterns.

In pairs, students categorise these words according to stress pattern and write the words in the correct column on their stress pattern sheet. Then they write each word on a separate blank card.

Pairs can use dictionaries or ask for help to check the stress patterns they are not sure of.
Pairs swap cards with another pair and write the new words they receive under the correct stress pattern on their sheets.

e.g.   Pair A:

●●●	●●●	●●●●	●●●●	●●●●
policeman	Manchester	photographer	consequently	preparation
mistaken	robbery	available	wonderfully	situation
decisive	hairdresser	respectable	passionately	conversation
arrival	interesting	identity		
	vegetable	apparently		

Pairs now write sentences or a short story using as many of the words as they can within a certain time limit.
The words can be used in any order, but can only be used once.

e.g.   Pair A: A respectable photographer was having a conversation with a hairdresser about a robbery in a Manchester vegetable garden. Apparently no policeman was available to investigate the situation.

Pairs read their sentences or story to the class and get a point for each of the words they use.

Alternative:

In pairs, students make up sentences but each word used in a sentence must come from a different stress category.
Pairs try to include all five of the categories in one sentence.

e.g.   A policeman in Manchester arrested a photographer after a conversation which was passionately intense.
A respectable hairdresser was consequently mistaken in his understanding of the situation.

What can you hear?
(Groups)

Photocopiable material: pp. 212-213

Focus: General phonology

Level: Intermediate

Time: 30'+

Materials: Board, counters, cards, die/spinner

Procedure:

Students play in groups of three.

Give each group a copy of the board, set of symbol cards, counters, and die/spinner.

Students prepare the cards by writing words on the back of the symbol cards that fit the tasks below. The symbols or initials on the back of the photocapiable cards identify the different tasks. Students place their counters in the bottom left corner of the board and take turns to spin/roll to see how many squares to advance. Play moves clockwise around the board.

When they've completed the outer ring of the board, they move to the next inner ring (following the arrows) until they have reached the centre (home) square.

e.g. Student A lands on a symbol, picks up the top card of the same symbol pile and performs the task on the card with the student on their right (student B). If the task is completed correctly, both students (A & B) move one space forward. If not, student C tries to complete the task with student A.

Student A can only move forward one square if another student can complete the task with them. Play then goes to student B. Each symbol card is associated with a different task.

TASKS: **ST - ✗**
Stress - Student A picks up a card and spells the word to student B.
Student B writes down the word and decides on which syllable the main stress goes.

INT - ✔
Intonation - Student A picks up a card and reads the statement on the card using the intonation in brackets. Student B must guess how student A feels.

SS - 👂
Same Sounds - Student A picks up a card and reads out the word. Student B must come up with two more words which rhyme with that word.

N - 📣
Things which make noise - Student A picks up a card, reads the word silently and tries to make a noise associated with the object/animal etc. Student B must guess what makes that noise.

C - ?
Chance squares - When a student lands on a chance square, they pick up a chance card and follow the instructions on the card.

TT - ☺
Tongue Twisters (Home) - When a student lands in the centre square (Home), they pick up a Tongue Twister card, read it silently, and then say it three times at normal speed with no mistakes or hesitations in order to win the game. If a student cannot say the Tongue Twister correctly, they spin/roll and go back that number of spaces.

Sample Cards:

ST - ✗ =	responsible	necessary
INT - ✔ =	You must be joking! (disbelieving)	I suppose so. (bored)
SS - 👂 =	round	make
N - 📣 =	trumpet	drill
C - ? =	move back 1 space	miss a turn
TT - ☺ =	Fry fresh fish	Red lorry, yellow lorry

ST - ✗ **INT - ✔**

SS - 👂 **N - 📣**

C - ? **TT - ☺**

Sound Shapes
(Groups)

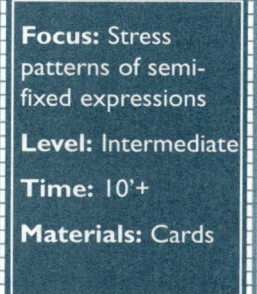

Photocopiable material: p. 214

Focus: Stress patterns of semi-fixed expressions

Level: Intermediate

Time: 10'+

Materials: Cards

Procedure:

Students play in groups of three.
Prepare sets of 5 sentence cards and 5 matching stress cards for each student in a group.
Each sentence card has two sentences. The second is a possible response to the first and is from 1 to 7 words long. Each stress card represents the stress pattern of the second sentence on each sentence card.

e.g. **Sentence Card:**

> *Life's really expensive these days.*
> *I know what you mean.*

Stress Card:

Shuffle the cards and give each student 5 sentence cards and 5 stress cards. The students read their cards silently and try to match the second sentence on their cards to one of their stress cards. When they have a match, they put them down as pairs.
For the unmatched cards, students take it in turns to read out the second sentence to the rest of the group as it would be said in response to the first sentence. Any student who thinks they have the corresponding stress card hands it over to the first student to make a pair.

e.g. **Card:**

> *Life's really expensive these days.*
> *I know what you mean.*

Student A: I *know* what you *mean.*

Student C: Has the stress card  and gives it to student A to make a pair.

It is now student B's turn to say the second sentence of one of their unmatched cards.
The winner is the first to put down all their cards.

Sample Cards:

> *I've got to go now.*
> *See you later.*

> *The door was left unlocked last night. Don't blame me!*

> *Can I bring some friends?*
> *The more the merrier.*

> *Can you help me for a minute?*
> *Of course!*

Extension:

Students write another similarly stressed expression under the one they have picked up:

That's *not* what I *meant.*
You *shouldn't* have told.

Not bad really.
Best time ever.

Limericks
(Group)

☞ **Pointer:**

Limericks are an interesting and fun way to stress rhyme and rhythm in the English language.

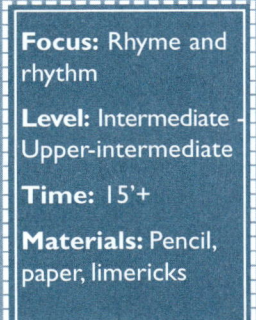

Focus: Rhyme and rhythm

Level: Intermediate - Upper-intermediate

Time: 15'+

Materials: Pencil, paper, limericks

Procedure:

Students play in groups of three.

Limericks are silly 5 line poems, which always follow the same rhyme and stress pattern: AABBA for the rhyme and 33223 for the number of stresses per line.

Read out a few sample limericks to the students. Have students repeat the limericks and give them a copy of one with the stress and rhyme pattern marked so they get the general idea.

Then, in groups of three, students complete one or more of the chosen tasks.

The class votes for the best one.

Sample Limericks:

```
        (1)        (2)        (3)
There was a young lady from Crewe,        (A)
        (1)      (2)       (3)
Who never knew quite what to do.          (A)
             (1)       (2)
She wore boots while in bed,              (B)
          (1)      (2)
With a sock on her head,                  (B)
          (1)       (2)       (3)
And drank lemonade out of her shoe.       (A)
```

Another young man had a feather,
And would dress head to toe all in leather.
He would tickle his nose,
Whenever he chose,
And said it's because of the weather.

The person we're next going to meet,
Would never wear shoes on his feet.
Whatever the season,
He gave just one reason,
It wasn't because of the heat.

Various Tasks/Ideas:

1 Take away the last word of each line except the first. Students guess what the missing words are.

e.g.
There was a young lady from Crewe,
Who never knew quite what to ....
She wore boots while in ....

2 Mix up the lines of two or more Limericks. Students rearrange them into the originals.

e.g.
He would tickle his nose,
Who never knew quite what to do.
And said it's because of the weather.

3 Take away the second and third lines. Students compose their own.

e.g.
There was a young lady from Crewe,
....
....
With a sock on her head,
And drank lemonade out of her shoe.

4 Mix up all the words from one Limerick. Students rearrange them into the original.

e.g.
She wore boots while in bed,
And drank lemonade out of her shoe.
Who never knew quite what to do.

5 Give alternative words which do not fit the rhyme or stress patterns. Students identify the wrong word.

e.g.
There was a young lady from Timbuktu/Crewe,
Who never knew/realised quite what to do.
She wore overcoats/boots while in bed,

6 Give only the stressed syllables. Students try to provide those missing.

e.g.
was ..... lady ..... Crewe
never ..... quite ..... do
boots ... . bed

7 Give students the first line of a Limerick. They then compose their own Limerick.

e.g.
There was a young lady from Crewe,
Who always dyed her hair blue.
She had rings on her fingers,   etc.

What do you mean exactly?
17 (Groups)

Photocopiable material: p. 215

Focus: Matching stress to meaning

Level: Intermediate

Time: 15'+

Materials: Cards

Procedure:

Students play in groups of three.
Photocopy or prepare sets of sentence cards for each group.
Each card has a sentence with one word stressed and an implied meaning in brackets.

Give the class examples and elicit how changing the sentence stress can change the meaning.

e.g.
He didn't eat **all** the cake. - (He did eat **some** of it.)
He didn't eat all the cake. - (This implies that **somebody else** did.)
He didn't eat all the **cake.** - (This implies that he did eat all of **something else.**)

Give each group a set of 20 cards which they place face down on the table.
Student A picks up a card and reads the sentence aloud, emphasising the word in **bold**, but does **not** read the words in brackets.

The other students in the group take turns guessing the meaning of the sentence from the stress.
The first student who guesses the meaning wins a point.

After all the cards have been used, the winner is the student with the most points.
Students can then prepare their own game cards.

Sample Cards:

I told you to turn **left** at the second traffic lights. (Not right.)	Why don't **you** cook for a change? (I always cook.)	He didn't tell **me** why. (But he told someone else.)
Tuesday is all right with **me.** (But what about you?)	But what do **you** think? (I know what I think.)	I can't really talk to you **now.** (But maybe later.)
You actually **liked** living there? (You didn't hate it?)	You don't believe me. (But others do.)	The **dessert** was great. (But not the main course.)
The accident wasn't **my** fault. (But it was the other driver's.)	Well, the **price** was better than I'd expected. (But the quality wasn't.)	He liked the film. (But I didn't.)

114

Sounds like ...?
18 (Pairs)

Photocopiable material: p. 216

Photocopiable material: p. 216

☞ **Pointer:**

Get students to find, collect and bring to class various pictures.

Focus: Individual sounds

Level: Intermediate

Time: 10'+

Materials: Cards, pictures, pencil, paper

Procedure:

Students play in pairs.
Prepare a set of word cards, each with a different sound highlighted in bold.
Choose pictures from class textbooks, magazines, cartoons, etc which have a lot of detail or action.

Give each pair a different picture and a set of word cards face down between them.
Student A picks up a word card, turns it over and both students individually write as many words containing that sound as they can find in their picture within a time limit (e.g. one minute).
The winner of the round is the one with the most words which their partner has not found.
Student B then picks up another word card with a different highlighted sound. The game continues with the same picture.

e.g.

Card: paint

Student A: Pasta, ~~potatoes~~, shop assistant, ~~shampoo~~, push-chair, people
Student B: ~~Potatoes~~, ~~shampoo~~, apples, pears, peppers

Student A has found four words/objects different from student B. Student B has found three.
Student A scores four points and student B scores three points.

Sample Cards:

shoe	tree	fire	lake	boat	garden
chair	jam	nose	rain	water	sun

6 Texts

Bear Hunt
(Class)

☞ **Pointer:**

Simple participation stories can be used to focus on different aspects of language.
e.g. prepositions of place, movement, etc.
Find stories in books or make them up yourself.

Focus: Vocabulary building, story telling

Level: Beginner - Pre-intermediate

Time: 10'+

Materials: Text

Procedure:

Choose a story or make one up with the language you wish to practise.

Tell the story – preferably from memory - using actions and sounds to illustrate each phrase.
Put a simple drawing for each of the places mentioned in the story on the board or use an overhead projector.   e.g. river, hill, forest, cave,   etc.

Students listen and join in by repeating the sounds and doing the actions.
Tell the story again, encouraging students to join in as best as they can with the words.
The third time say as little as needed, encouraging the students to tell the whole story themselves with sounds and actions.

e.g. We're all going on a bear hunt.
We are brave and we are strong.
We're not afraid.
We go through the long grass (swish, swish)
Across the river (splash, splash)
Up the hill (phew, phew)
Down the hill (wheee, wheee)
Into the dark forest (hoo, hoo)
Out of the dark forest (ahh, ahh)
Oh, here's a cave
Let's go in
It's very dark! (oohh, oohh)
Oh! What's this!
It's very furry… and very warm… and very big… and it's waking up!
Oh no! It's a bear!
Quick! Let's go!
We go out of the cave
Into the dark forest
Out of the dark forest
Up the hill (phew, phew)
Down the hill (wheee, wheee)
Across the river (splash, splash)
Through the long grass (swish, swish)
Into the house
Lock the door (click, click)
And all jump into bed
We're safe! (wheww)

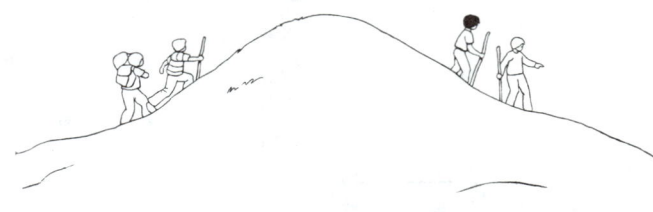

Extension:

In groups, students make up their own story with actions and present it to the class.

Action Songs
2 (Class)

Photocopiable material: p. 217

Focus: Associating actions with words

Level: Beginner - Elementary

Time: 10'+

Materials: Song lyrics

Procedure:

Students perform actions to such well-known songs as:

The wheels of the bus	Head & shoulders	This is the way we wash our face
If you're happy and you know it	Incey Wincey Spider	

Write the words of the song on the board or use an overhead projector and transparency. Have students push their desks back and stand in a circle in the middle of the room. Sing each line of the song with appropriate actions and get students to repeat. Students then sing the whole song with the actions.

e.g.   Students touch the parts of the body with both hands as they sing or chant the words.

Head & shoulders, knees and toes, knees and toes.
Head & shoulders, knees and toes, knees and toes.
And eyes and ears and mouth and nose,
Head & shoulders, knees and toes, knees and toes!

This song leads nicely into Musical Statues
As the students are singing and performing the actions, stop the music (or say *Stop!*).
Students have to hold the position they are in when the music stops– like a statue. Any student who moves before you start the music again (or say *Go!*) is out and helps you judge who moves the next time.
When a student moves you have to tell them why they are out. e.g. '*You moved your elbow.*'
The winner is the last person left who didn't move when the music stopped.

Rounds
3 (Class)

Photocopiable material: p. 217

Focus: Learning phrase patterns through song

Level: Elementary-Pre-intermediate

Time: 10'+

Materials: Song lyrics

Procedure:

Divide the class into two groups. Choose a well known round such as:

Row, row, row your boat	London's burning	Brother John
London Bridge is falling down	Twinkle, twinkle little star	

Write the words of the song on the board or use an overhead projector and transparency.
Sing each line of the round and have students repeat after you. Put the first two lines together and repeat, and then the last two. Finally, sing the whole round and have students repeat.

Row, row, row your boat
Gently down the stream
Merrily, merrily, merrily, merrily
Life is but a dream

The class repeats the round a few times until they are familiar with it.
Explain to the class that the the first group will start the round and when they get to the end of the second line, group two will begin singing the round from the beginning. Both groups continue singing the round 3 times through without stopping.
With groups who are fairly confident, the class can be divided into 4 groups.
The song can go on for as long as you want.

Cumulative Songs
4 (Class)

Photocopiable material: pp. 218-219

Focus: Learning sentence patterns through song

Level: Pre-intermediate-Intermediate

Time: 10' +

Materials: Song lyrics

Procedure:

Photocopy the song with the blanks and give each student a copy.
The first two verses are the refrain and are repeated throughout the song. Sing/say each line and have the students repeat. Then say both verses together and students repeat a couple of times to get the rhythm.
Write the key words to the song on the board.

Go through the song and ask the students to fill in the blank spaces using the key words and the same pattern as the first two verses. Explain that the key words will rhyme with a part of the song. Give a few examples and check to make sure they have filled in the blanks correctly.
Now, start with the first verse and have students join in and sing/say the whole song.

e.g.

There was an old woman who swallowed a fly,
I don't know why she swallowed a fly,
Perhaps she'll die.

There was an old woman who swallowed a spider,
That wriggled and jiggled and tickled inside her,
She swallowed the spider to catch the fly,
I don't know why she swallowed a fly,
Perhaps she'll die.

There was an old woman who swallowed *a bird*,
How absurd! To swallow *a bird*.
She swallowed the *bird* to catch the spider,
That wriggled and jiggled and tickled inside her,
She swallowed the spider to catch the fly,
I don't know why she swallowed a fly,
Perhaps she'll die.

There was an old woman who swallowed a cat,
Imagine that! *to swallow a cat*,
She *swallowed the cat* to catch the *bird*,
She *swallowed the bird* to catch the *spider*,
That wriggled and jiggled and tickled inside her,
She swallowed the spider to catch the fly,
I don't know why she swallowed a fly,
Perhaps she'll die.   etc.

Key Words
fly
spider
bird
cat
dog
goat
cow
horse

Variation:

Go through the refrain with the students and act-out/mime the animals before you say them. e.g. *fly, spider*
Have the students guess what the animal is and then repeat the line with you. Go through the song in this way once, and then do it again to see how many animals the students remember.

Cumulative Song examples:
Ten green bottles hanging on the wall   There were ten in the bed and the little one said, 'Roll over!'

Rhythmic Poems
5 (Class)

Photocopiable material: p. 217

Photocopiable material: p. 217

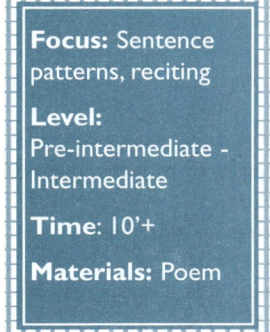

Focus: Sentence patterns, reciting

Level: Pre-intermediate - Intermediate

Time: 10'+

Materials: Poem

> ☞ **Pointer:**
>
> Anthologies of poetry for children normally have plenty of illustrations which you can use to stimulate interest and understanding.

Procedure:

Divide the class into two groups.
Photocopy and give students a copy of the poem and explain/elicit any unknown vocabulary.
Start a clapping rhythm - 4 claps per line - and say the poem aloud keeping in time to the rhythm.
Say the poem a second time and ask the students to underline the stressed words.
Get the class to clap with you. When they are used to the rhythm say the first line of the poem and have the class repeat it after you. Go through the poem line by line in this way and then have the class repeat the whole poem.

e.g.   The <u>best</u> little <u>animal's</u> a <u>tiny</u> <u>mouse</u>.
You can <u>find</u> it in a <u>field</u>. You can <u>find</u> it in your <u>house</u>.
They <u>frighten</u> great big <u>elephants</u> but <u>they</u> don't fr ghten <u>me</u>.
I <u>often</u> have a <u>party</u> and <u>invite</u> them in for <u>tea</u>.

Have the two groups face each other. As the students keep the clapping rhythm go ng, group A will start with the first line of the poem and group B will then say the second, group A the third and finally group B the last line.
Repeat, having group B say the first line.

e.g.   Group A: The <u>best</u> little <u>animal's</u> a <u>tiny</u> <u>mouse</u>.
Group B: You can <u>find</u> it in a <u>field</u>, you can <u>find</u> it in your <u>house</u>.
Group A: They <u>frighten</u> great big <u>elephants</u> but <u>they</u> don't <u>frighten</u> <u>me</u>.
Group B: I <u>often</u> have a <u>party</u> and <u>invite</u> them in for <u>tea</u>.

Extension:

Students can also write their own four line verses and poems.

e.g   The <u>worst</u> little <u>animal's</u> a <u>nasty</u> <u>fly</u>.
It can <u>bite</u> you on your <u>nose</u>, it can <u>bite</u> you on your <u>eye</u>.
They <u>often</u> wake me <u>up</u> when I'm <u>sleeping</u> in my <u>bed</u>.
I <u>wish</u> they'd all go <u>far</u> away and <u>bother</u> you <u>instead</u>!

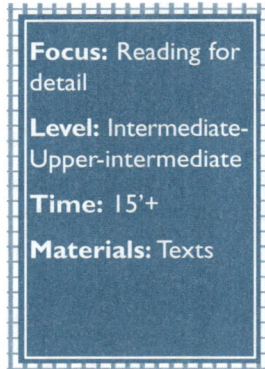

Correct it!
(Groups)

Focus: Reading for detail

Level: Intermediate-Upper-intermediate

Time: 15'+

Materials: Texts

Procedure:

Students play in groups of three. (Try to make an even number of groups.)

Each group chooses a different text of no more than 100 words from their course book, a newspaper or a magazine.

In groups, students rewrite their text, removing ten words and replacing them with others of the same type. Students underline the words they have changed. The words must fit logically so that the adapted text makes sense.

Groups exchange texts. Each group reads the adapted text, discusses it and comes up with a list of what they think the original words were before being changed.

The groups that exchanged texts get together and read out the lists they have made. Groups get one point for words that are the same as in the original text.

The group with the most points wins.

Original text: *If you have ever dreamt about <u>incredibly</u> big seas with huge <u>powerful</u> waves crashing onto <u>sandy</u> beaches, then you should <u>definitely</u> think about learning to surf. It's the most <u>exciting</u> water sport there is. <u>Serious</u> surfers must be very <u>brave</u>, love adventure and have lots of energy. Once they have <u>experienced</u> the excitement of a ride on <u>top</u> of the waves, they <u>never</u> want to stop.*   (From "Enterprise 4")

Adapted text: If you have ever dreamt about <u>really</u> big seas with huge <u>strong</u> waves crashing onto <u>clean</u> beaches, then you should <u>certainly</u> think about learning to surf. It's the most <u>wonderful</u> water sport there is. <u>Good</u> surfers must be very <u>fit</u>, love adventure and have lots of energy. Once they have <u>felt</u> the excitement of a ride on <u>one</u> of the waves, they <u>rarely</u> want to stop.

Alternatives:

In groups, students replace words with others that fit grammatically, but do not fit logically.
Students do not underline the words they replace.

e.g.   If you have ever dreamt about *frightened* big seas with huge powerful *fish* crashing onto sandy *rocks*, then you should *once* think about learning to surf. It's the most *boring* water sport there is. *Silly* surfers must be *nearly* brave, love adventure and have lots of *friends*. Once they have experienced the excitement of a *flight* on top of the waves, they never want to *swim*.

Give criteria for which words to change - Verbs, adverbs, adjectives, nouns or prepositions

Variation:

Use quotations, lines from songs or poems and change three or four words:

'If Cleopatra's <u>nose</u> had been <u>shorter</u>, the whole <u>face</u> of the <u>earth</u> would have changed.' (Pascal)
'If Cleopatra's <u>feet</u> had been <u>dirtier</u>, the whole <u>surface</u> of the <u>carpet</u> would have changed.

'If a picture <u>paints</u> a thousand <u>words</u>, then why can't I <u>paint</u> you?'
'If a picture <u>draws</u> a thousand <u>balloons</u>, then why can't I <u>imagine</u> you?

Parallel Texts
(Pairs)

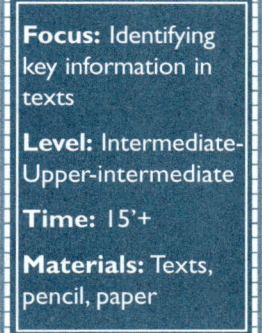

Focus: Identifying key information in texts

Level: Intermediate-Upper-intermediate

Time: 15'+

Materials: Texts, pencil, paper

Procedure:

Students play in pairs. Two pairs play against each other.

Choose two texts or news items, dealing with the same topic, taken from two different newspapers or magazines. Label one text A and the other B.

Give pair A text A, and pair B text B.

Pairs read their texts and come up with 6 questions that can be answered by the text and write them on a piece of paper in the form of a questionnaire.

Each question begins with one of the question words: who, what, where, when, why, how.

On the text, students underline the answers to the questions they have written.

Pair A swaps their questionnaire with pair B.

Pairs try to answer the questions on the questionnaire using the information in the text they have.

Pairs return the questionnaires to the original pairs who check the information, referring to the answers they have in their original text.

The winning pair is the one who answers the most questions correctly.

e.g.

Questions (from text A)	Answers (from text B)
Who *are Sil, Cam and Lo?*	*A girl trio from Portugal called Da Mustard.*
What *are they going to do?*	*They are going on a tour.*
Where *are they going to play?*	*In 25 countries on three continents.*
When *are they going to start touring?*	*They will start touring April 1st.*
Why *is the older sister amazed?*	*???*
How *did they become famous?*	*They had a number one hit song.*

Sample texts:

Text A	Text B
Sil, Cam and Lo, <u>otherwise known as Da Mustard, are to go on the road</u> after the phenomenal success of their first single, which reached number 1 in 18 countries. The have apparently got an album near completion and will be showcasing this on their <u>three month tour, starting in Europe in the Spring, and moving on to Asia and Australia.</u> When asked what it was like to become an overnight sensation, Sil, the older sister, said, 'It's just amazing really. I can't believe it! When <u>we won Pop Idol in Lisbon</u> we never thought we would become <u>so internationally famous.</u>'	Da Mustard, the girl trio from Portugal, who inexplicably had half the world doing their dance moves while singing along to nonsense words, have announced that they are to tour starting April the 1st. They have been booked to play an amazing 25 countries on three continents. The teenage sisters may, however, have difficulty filling an evening as they have only ever recorded the one song – 'hedameca choota boo'. But as the CD has eight versions of the same thing, they could probably please their likely audience of young girls by just repeating the same song.

Report Writing
(Pairs)

Focus: Preparing and answering questionnaires, short report writing

Level: Intermediate-Upper-intermedeiate

Time: 20'+

Materials: Pencil, paper

Procedure:

Students play in pairs.

Have each pair prepare a multiple-choice questionnaire. Each questionnaire should have the same number of questions. The topics can be related to material recently studied in their coursework, current affairs relevant to their community or more general questions.

Pairs set up and write their questionnaire and then under the 'Me' column, make a prediction of what they think the majority of the class will answer.

Each pair presents their questionnaire to the class, giving the question/topic and the four possible choices. Students raise their hands to indicate which one they think is correct and the presenting pair puts a tick for each vote in the correct box.

If the prediction made by the pair under the 'Me' column agrees with the majority of the class, they get a point. After all the pairs have presented their questionnaires, the one with the most correct predictions is the winner.

e.g.

Questions	Me	A	B	C	D
Most widespread illness	A	Cancer ✓✓✓✓	Asthma ✓✓✓	Cholera ✓	Influenza ✓✓
Best way to lose weight	A	eat only fruit	exercise	eat every 2nd day	don't eat sweets
Most common injury	C	leg	arm	back	head
Most common ache	A	head	tooth	stomach	back
Best breakfast	C	eggs	cereal	fruit	croissant
Best exercise	B	aerobics	swimming	cycling	jogging

Pair A: What do you think is the most widespread illness - A-Cancer, B-Asthma, C-Cholera or D-Influenza?

Pair A gets a point for correctly guessing that cancer would get more votes than any other option.

In pairs, the students now write a report based on the information they gathered from their questionnaire.

Students use phrases such as: The majority..., 75% of the class..., Two thirds..., a few..., a small minority..., Everybody/Nobody felt that..., It is clear that..., etc.

Possible questions:
most difficult sport to play
best ice cream flavour
best colour for a car

easiest thing to draw
favourite types of transport
best time of day

Witness (1)
(Groups)

Photocopiable material: p. 220

Focus: Recalling details, writing

Level: Intermediate-Upper-intermediate

Time: 15'+

Materials: Picture, short video clip, pencil, paper

Procedure:

Students play in groups of three.

Show the class a picture with a lot of detail or a short video of an incident for thirty seconds.

Give students five minutes to individually write sentences detailing what they saw.

In groups, students exchange information and write a collective paragraph based on the details they have noted and agree on.

Groups exchange paragraphs. Show students the picture or video again.

Groups check the information with the picture/video and put a tick for every correct action in the paragraph in front of them. They add up the ticks and give the paragraph back to the original group.

The group with the most points wins.

Witness (2)
(Pairs)

Focus: Predicting, writing

Level: Intermediate-Upper-intermediate

Time: 15'+

Materials: Pictures, pencil, paper

Procedure:

Students play in pairs.

Find two identical magazine pictures with plenty of detail or action in them.

Cut up one of the pictures so that you have the same number of pieces as there are pairs in the class.

Give a piece of the picture to each pair.

Give pairs five minutes to discuss and write notes about what they would expect to see in the whole picture.

Pairs read out their notes to the class. Show the whole picture to the class. The pair with the most accurate details is the winner.

Alternative 1:

Give each pair a different picture and tell them not to let anyone else see it.

Pairs tear off a section of the picture. Each pair writes a list of 10 words or phrases about what is in the rest of the picture – 5 facts are true and 5 facts are false. The true and false items should be in a mixed up order.

Pairs exchange their lists and picture sections and then tick which of the 5 items on the list they think are true about the picture. Pairs read to each other the 5 words/phrases they have ticked and get a point for each correct one. Pairs show each other the rest of their pictures. The pair with the most ticks is the winner.

Alternative 2:

Place sets of similar pictures, e.g. postcards of different beach scenes, people or architecture, face up on the table.

Each student writes a short description of one of the pictures.

Students swap their descriptions and try to guess which picture has been described.

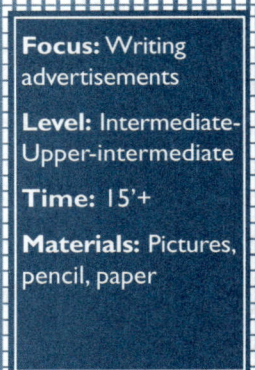

It's a whatsit!
11 (Pairs)

Focus: Writing advertisements

Level: Intermediate-Upper-intermediate

Time: 15'+

Materials: Pictures, pencil, paper

Procedure:

Students play in pairs.

Ask students to bring in pictures of various products cut out from magazines and cut off any text on the pictures. Give each pair one of the pictures.

Pairs write an advertising blurb with a maximum of 20 words (without mentioning the name or exact type of product) to accompany their picture.

Pairs take it in turns to read out their blurbs to the class. The rest of the pairs get 10 seconds to agree with their partner on what they think the product is and write it down. In turns, pairs read out their guesses. The presenting pair then tells them what it is and shows the picture. Each pair with a correct guess gets a point.

The pair with the most points after every pair has had a turn is the winner.

Example blurb: *There's no time like the present and there's no present like the time.* (A watch).

Alternative:

Elicit from students sets of products which are similar and write them on the board.

Pairs choose one product from any set and write a blurb for that item without mentioning the actual product.

Pairs take it in turns to read their blurbs to the class who guess what the product is. Each correct guess gets a point.

Example sets:

toothbrush, toothpick, mouthwash, floss, toothpaste, chewing gum
pullover, fleece, shirt, cardigan, jeans, jacket
sports car, family car, van, motorbike, bicycle
coffee, cola, water, tea, fruit drink, milk

───

Rapid Writing
12 (Class)

> ☞ **Pointer:**
>
> Time alloted for writing the continuation should depend on the level of the class.

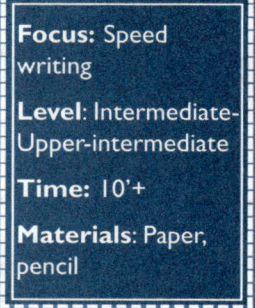

Focus: Speed writing

Level: Intermediate-Upper-intermediate

Time: 10'+

Materials: Paper, pencil

Procedure:

Dictate a start off sentence to the class. Students write this sentence on a piece of paper.

Students then have 30 seconds to write a continuation to the story starting on the next line.

At the end of 30 seconds, say *'TIME'* and the students must stop writing even if they are in the middle of a word.

Each student folds their paper so that only the last line of writing is showing and passes it to the student on their right. Each student now has a new piece of paper with just one line showing. Students have to continue the story based on that line. Continue in this way until the papers are full.

At the end of the process, each student unfolds the paper they are holding and reads the story to the class.

The class votes on the most interesting / amusing story.

e.g.   Starting sentence: It was a beautiful day but it didn't end that way.
Student A: Karen was sitting in the garden wondering...
Student B: what she was going to do that day. Just then, she saw...
Student C: her brother, Ken, walking towards her carrying something ... etc.

Story Building
(Groups)

13

Photocopiable material: p. 221

Focus: Collaborative story writing

Level: Intermediate-Upper-intermediate

Time: 20'+

Materials: Cards

Procedure:

Students play in groups of three.

Photocopy or prepare 'story type' cards and write a list of connectors on the board.

Give each student 15 blank word cards. Students write five different verbs, five different nouns and five different adjectives each one on an individual card.

Students in each group put their cards together, shuffle them and spread them out face down on the table. Each group turns over 25 of the word cards and removes the rest from the table.

Give each group a different 'story type' card.

Groups have ten minutes to use all the words they have turned face up to write a story based on their 'story type'. Students can use connectors from the list on the board and also other words not on the cards.

When the ten minutes are up, groups take it in turns to read out their stories to the class.

The class votes for the best story.

Connectors: so, next, then, after, meanwhile, consequently, because, but, if, while, who, which, etc

Story type cards: | folk tale | science fiction | comedy | adventure | fantasy | horror |

Sample Cards:

Verbs: | break | eat | drive | return | change | shake |

Nouns: | island | tree | letter | ship | castle | jungle |

Adjectives: | dark | strange | golden | narrow | beautiful | amazing |

Alternative:

Instead of 'story type' cards, give groups 'start line' cards.

Sample Cards:

| It was a dark and stormy night... | The only clue was the broken window. | Once upon a time... | He gazed longingly out the window. |

| You wouldn't believe me if I told you there are little green people living in my garden. | He seemed to have everything you could hope for, but he had a dark secret. | Suddenly, right in front of us, was the most beautiful waterfall we had ever seen. |

Key Words
14 (Pairs)

☞ **Pointers:**
- This type of activity can also be done individually or in small groups.
- Longer texts may be used with more advanced students.

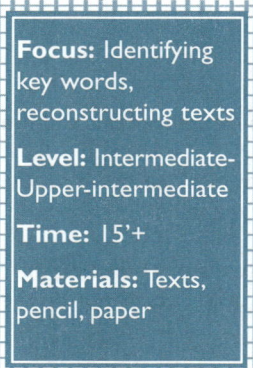

Focus: Identifying key words, reconstructing texts

Level: Intermediate-Upper-intermediate

Time: 15'+

Materials: Texts, pencil, paper

Procedure:

Students play in pairs. Two pairs play against each other.

Give each pair a different short text (not more than 50 words) taken from a book, magazine or newspaper. In pairs, students read the text and decide on and underline the key words.

The key words should include proper nouns and be no more than 30% of the total number of words in the text.

Two pairs play together and one pair tries to reconstruct the other pair's text.

Pair A dictates their key words to pair B.

Pair B asks pair A a maximum of ten yes/no questions to find out information.

Pair B now dictates their key words to pair A who asks ten yes/no questions about pair B's text to get information.

Using the information they have learned, pairs try to write a version of the original text using all the key words that were dictated and filling in any others they think are missing.

Pairs read their versions and score one point for every extra word they write that is the same as the word in the original.

e.g.   Pair A key words:

'cold ... morning ... Harry ... dog ... Sam ... fireplace ... kitchen ... sister ... outside ... snowman ... friends ...'

Pair B: *Is Harry a young boy?*
Pair A: *Yes.*
Pair B: *Is Sam Harry's brother?*
Pair A: *No.*
Pair B: *Is Sam the name of Harry's dog?*
Pair A: *Yes.*
Pair B: *Is the fireplace in the kitchen?*
Pair A: *Yes.*
Pair B: *Is the sister in the kitchen?*
Pair A: *No.*   etc

Pair B's version of the original text:

It was a cold morning and Harry was playing with his dog, Sam, near the fireplace in the kitchen. His sister was outside making a snowman with her friends. **(9 points)**

Finally pairs compare their written versions with the original texts to check accuracy of information and language:

One cold winter morning, Harry and his dog, Sam, were sitting by the fireplace. in the kitchen. His sister was outside building a snowman with her friends.

Trilma Headlines

(Pairs)

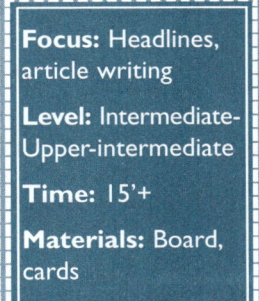

Photocopiable material: p. 222

Focus: Headlines, article writing

Level: Intermediate-Upper-intermediate

Time: 15'+

Materials: Board, cards

Procedure:

Students play in pairs.

Have students write 6 headlines each on double-sided cards (9 blank cards). The headlines should have three words in them and have the pattern - noun, verb, noun.   e.g. MAN BITES DOG

The students write each word of a headline on an individual card. They turn the cards over and write each word of a new headline on the other side, making sure the nouns are written on the back of other noun cards and the verbs on the back of verb cards. e.g. On the back of MAN a student might write QUEEN and on the back of BITES a student might write LEAVES.

Collect all the cards from the students, shuffle them and give each pair a board and each student 4 noun cards and 4 verb cards.

On the board write: When? Where? How? Why? What happened next?

Student A starts by putting 3 cards on the 3 spaces along the top of the outer frame on the game board to make a headline.

e.g. ELEPHANT BECOMES PRESIDENT

Student A must now use the question words written on the board to make up a story to go with the headline.

Student B now turns over one of the noun cards on the board to show a new noun, (e.g turns over ELEPHANT to reveal SHIP) puts down a verb card and noun card in the spaces below to make a new headline and also tells a story using the question words.

Student A repeats this procedure for the spaces along the bottom. There is now only one space left on the outer frame, so student B turns over the 2 noun cards and puts down a verb card to complete the headline and tells a story using the question words.

Student B continues the game by placing a completed headline on the top 3 spaces of the inner frame and telling a story. When this frame is completed, the students turn over any verb card and place it in the centre space. Pairs use this centre verb card and any two of the nouns diagonally connected to it to make a headline. Students may use the nouns on the other side of the diagonal cards. Pairs use the questions on the board to write an article to go with the headline. Pairs present their articles to the class who votes for the most original one.

Sample board:

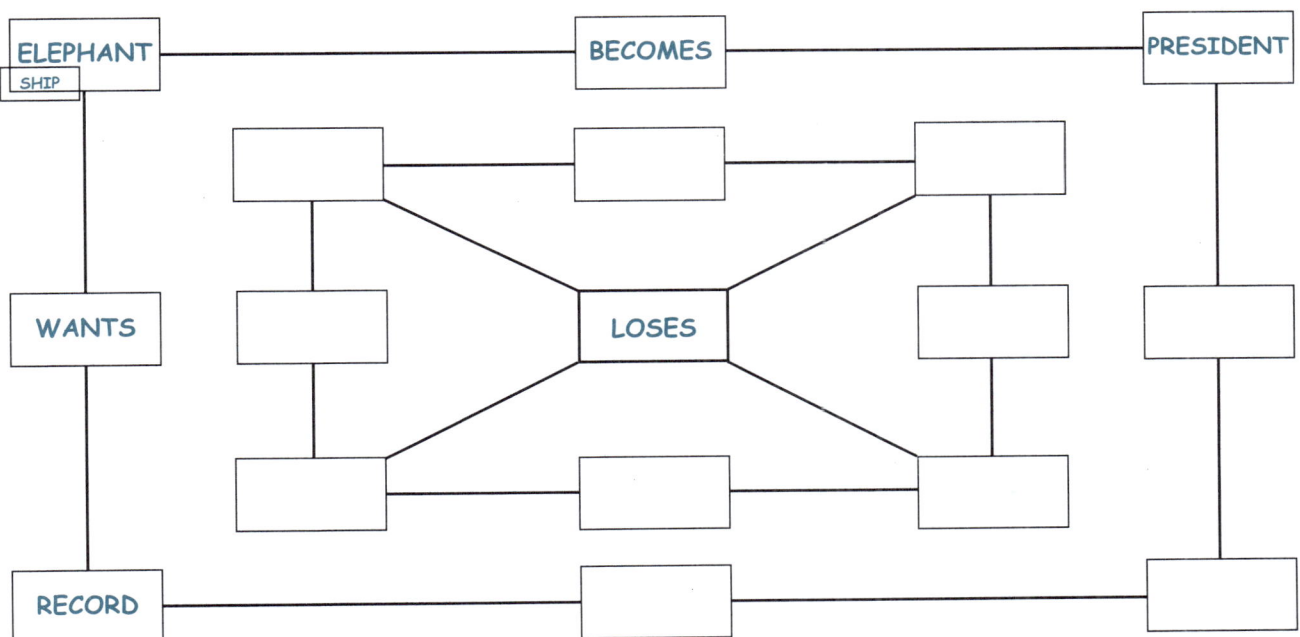

That's better!
16 (Groups)

Photocopiable material: p. 223

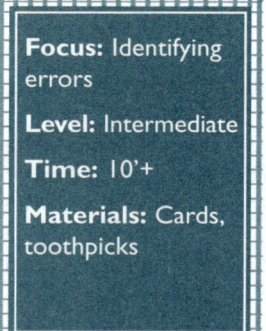

Focus: Identifying errors

Level: Intermediate

Time: 10'+

Materials: Cards, toothpicks

> **☞ Pointer:**
>
> For this activity, it is a good idea to use sentences from the students' own written work to focus on frequent errors.

Procedure:

Students play in groups of three.

Prepare, or have each student write, ten sentence cards. Give each group a pile of toothpicks.

Five of the cards will have sentences with structural or lexical errors on them and five will be 'error-free' sentences. Students should put a tick (✓) next to their 'error-free' sentences and not show their cards to the other students.

If students write their own cards, check around the class for sentence accuracy and that they are ticking the right cards. Groups shuffle and exchange their cards with another group.

Students take it in turns to read out a sentence card. Any student in the group who thinks the sentence is correct, gives a thumbs up sign. Any student who thinks the sentence has an error, gives a thumbs down sign. The student reading the sentence reads it again and says whether it is correct or incorrect and also makes the thumbs up or thumbs down sign. The students who correctly said if the sentence contained an error or not get a toothpick.

If the sentence was an incorrect one, the student to the right of the student reading has a chance to put the sentence into correct English. If they do so, they get a toothpick. If not, the third student has a chance to win a toothpick by correcting the sentence. The winner is the student with the most toothpicks after everyone in the group has read out their cards.

e.g.   Student A: | I have long time to see you. |

Student B: 👍

Student C: 👎

Student A: *I have long time to see you. The sentence is incorrect.* 👎   (Student C gets a toothpick.)
Student B: *I haven't seen you for a long time.* (This is correct and student B gets a toothpick.)

Sample Cards:

<table>
<tr><td align="center">'Error' Cards</td><td align="center">'Error-free' Cards</td></tr>
<tr><td>I have long time to see you.</td><td>✓ What time do you think it is?</td></tr>
<tr><td>I lost the bus.</td><td>✓ You're getting on my nerves!</td></tr>
<tr><td>This is not tasting nice, no?</td><td>✓ Fancy a coffee?</td></tr>
<tr><td>Why wanting you this?</td><td>✓ If you will, I will!</td></tr>
<tr><td>Never I said this!</td><td>✓ We're off tomorrow.</td></tr>
</table>

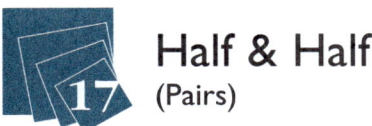

Half & Half
17 (Pairs)

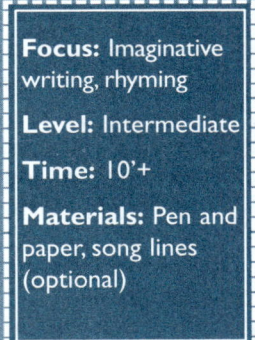

Focus: Imaginative writing, rhyming

Level: Intermediate

Time: 10'+

Materials: Pen and paper, song lines (optional)

Procedure:

Students play in pairs

Dictate the first line of a typical/real song. Students in pairs write it down and have one minute to compose and write the second line, which must rhyme with and have the same rhythm as the first. Dictate the third line - students compose the fourth, and so on.

e.g.

Teacher:	You are so good to me
Pair A:	You make me feel completely free
Teacher:	I will always remember you
Pair A:	I'll stay with you through rain and snow
Teacher:	You just make my life complete
Pair A:	Though you've got rather smelly feet
Teacher:	Through thick and thin, just wait and see
Pair A:	That's the way best friends should be!

Students read or sing their versions for the class.

Acrostics
18 (Pairs)

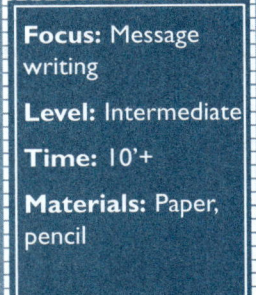

Focus: Message writing

Level: Intermediate

Time: 10'+

Materials: Paper, pencil

Procedure:

Students play in pairs.

Explain to the class that an acrostic is when the first or last letter of a list of words or phrases makes up a new word or phrase. In this case we will be taking existing words and making new phrases/messages.

Use the names of a couple of students as an example.

e.g.

| Mangos |
| Are |
| Really |
| Yummy |

| Martians |
| All |
| Read |
| Kafka |

In pairs the students choose a word (one of their names or a word out of their course books) and write it vertically.

Students use the letters of that word to create a small message or text. Ask students to see if they can make a message or text that is related to the original word. Students can use single words or phrases after each letter.

When students have come up with five acrostics, pairs take it in turns to read them out to the class who votes for the best ones.

e.g.

| Put words together |
| Occasionally |
| Even |
| Making |
| Sense |

| Washing on the beach |
| All foamy |
| Very |
| Exciting to |
| Swim in |

19 What's missing?
(Pairs)

Focus: Linking ideas, story writing

Level: Intermediate-Upper-intermediate

Time: 25'+

Materials: Pictures, paperclips

Procedure:

Students play in pairs.

Ask each student to find and cut out two pictures they like from a magazine. Each pair will have four pictures.

In pairs, students have five minutes to write the first paragraph of a story based on one of the pictures. Pairs paperclip their paragraph to the corresponding picture and pass them to the pair on their right. This pair looks at the picture, reads the paragraph in front of them and continues that story by writing the second paragraph based on one of their three remaining pictures.

Pairs exchange paragraphs again and write the the third paragraph, using one of their two remaining pictures. For the fourth paragraph, pairs use their last picture to write an ending to the story.

Pairs take it in turns to read the story to the class, one student reads the story and the other holds up the relevant picture for each paragraph.

The class votes on the best story.

---

20 Riddles
(Pairs)

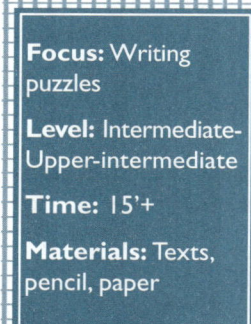

Photocopiable material: p. 224

Focus: Writing puzzles

Level: Intermediate-Upper-intermediate

Time: 15'+

Materials: Texts, pencil, paper

Procedure:

Students play in pairs.

Photocopy and give each pair the following puzzle or write it out on the board.

Go over the puzzle with the students, explaining that each sentence is a clue to a letter. When students have figured out the puzzle they will find a hidden word. Give a couple of examples so students understand the process. Allow pairs a few minutes to try and solve it.

e.g.

My 1st is in crash but not in smash.	(possible letters: c, r)
My 2nd is in crack but not in smack.	(possible letters: c, r)
My 3rd is in broke and also in smoke.	(possible letters: o, k, e)
My 4th is in kick but not in sink.	(possible lettes: c)
My 5th is in grow and also in show.	(possible letters: o, w)
My 6th is in made but not in make.	(possible letters: d)
My 7th is in fill and also in will.	(possible letters: i, l)
My 8th is in life but not in wife.	(possible letters: l)
My 9th is in Eve but not in Adam.	(possible letters: e, v)
What am I?	
	(Answer: crocodile)

Give each pair a different word, or have pairs choose a word of their own. Each word should have the same number of letters.

Pairs make up their own riddle and swap with another pair who have to try and solve it.

The pair who finds the hidden word first is the winner.

What happened?
21 (Pairs)

Focus: Reporting news, summarising

Level: Advanced

Time: 30'+

Materials: Articles, question cards

Procedure:

Students play in pairs.

Give each pair part of an English newspaper or magazine and tell them to choose an article that they find interesting. Each pair should have a different article.

Alternatively, articles could be grouped by section - international news, domestic, sports, business, entertainment, social etc. Each pair is given a topic section from which to choose an article.

Students highlight the key information and make a list of key words in the article.

Pairs then think of how to present the news from the article as if they were reading the news on television or giving a press conference.

One student in the class acts as scorekeeper and writes the names of the pairs on the board - pairs could choose to be called after rival news channels in their country.

Pairs take it in turns to stand at the front of the class and present their news item. They do not bring the article with them but use the list of keywords to help them.

Give each student in the class a card with one of these question words on it: Who? What? Where? When? Why? How?

One student in the pair begins telling the news based on the article they have read and highlighted. This student is the *newscaster*. The other student can help out if that student can't remember something important.

Any student in the class can interrupt the news at any time by holding up their question card and using the word on the card to ask a question requesting further information.

When the *newscaster* sees a card held up, they must stop and say, "Yes?". The student with the card then asks their question.

If a question is asked and the *newscaster* or their partner cannot provide the answer, the point goes to the pair who asked the question.

If the *newscaster* or their partner can answer the question, that team gets the point.

Sample text:

Paint it yellow (with lots of greenbacks)

The **Rolling Stones**, celebrating their **fortieth** year together, inaugurated their latest **world tour** by **flying** above **New York** yesterday in a huge yellow **balloon** emblazoned with their trademark red tongue. This tour, their first in three years, kicks off in **Boston** on **September** 5th, and will involve up to **300 people** being on the road for months.

They fly in a specially **converted 747**, but are playing several concerts in each country on the programme so they won't need to fly so often.

The band doesn't have a **new album** to promote, but with the compilation CD "**40 Licks**" doing so well, they can rely on their extensive back catalogue to bring the punters in and add to the **one billion dollars** they have earned **since 1989**. They already hold the **record** for the highest grossing concert tour ever with their **1994 tour**, which brought in **121 million dollars**. For Sir Mick and Co., the sky's the limit.

Key Words

Rolling Stones
fortieth
world tour
flying
New York
balloon
Boston
September
300 people
converted 747
new album
40 Licks
one billion dollars
since 1989
record
1994 tour
121 million dollars

Brushing your teeth	Changing a baby's nappy
Watching a horror film	Making a cake
Ironing a shirt	Planting a small tree
Riding a bicycle for the first time	Having an argument
Painting a picture	Standing in a queue for a long time
Watching an exciting football match	Frying eggs

Getting dressed	Washing clothes by hand
Cooking a meal	Hanging a picture on the wall
Making a brick wall	Planting a tree
Making a cup of tea	Changing the bed linen
Putting up a tent	Washing the dishes
Starting up a car	Painting a fence

doctor	teacher	accountant
model	dentist	shepherd
ballet dancer	singer	butcher
cook	air steward	politician
fireman	hairdresser	actor
baker	policeman	painter

frightened	Very tasty.
Keep quiet!	Don't move!
tired	We won!
Go away!	What's the time?
surprised	Come here.
hungry	I don't know.

bored	happy
worried	scared
cold	hot
in a hurry	irritated
sleepy	sad
depressed	uncomfortable

a busy businessman	someone carrying heavy shopping
a policeman on patrol	a pregnant woman
a two year old	an army officer
a famous singer	an old man
a clown	a top model
the Queen of England	a window shopper

There's no hot water.	The shower doesn't work.	There was no bread with breakfast.
There is a nasty smell in the room.	The room is freezing.	I want a room with a view.
The lift is broken.	The bathroom mirror is broken.	There are no towels in my room.
I want a double, not two single beds.	You have given me the wrong key.	There are no sheets on my bed.
The telephone does not work.	There is no shampoo.	There is a stranger in my room.
The television does not work.	There is no water in the swimming pool.	I have no electricity in my room.

Find someone who ...	Name	More information
has got a brother.		
has eggs for breakfast.		
has been abroad.		
rides a bicycle.		
lives in your street/area.		
can speak another language.		
wants to move house.		
has been to the cinema recently.		
knows where Timbuktu is.		
has broken a bone.		

Why is the sky blue?	Why does the sea have waves?	Why do we have dreams?
Why do we get colds?	Why is sand usually yellow?	Why do most people live in the city?
Why do the British drive on the left side of the road?	Why do people climb mountains?	Why do people say owls are wise?
Why are stop signs and fire engines red?	Why can't penguins fly?	Why do bears sleep in the winter?
Why is the sea salty?	Why does everyone want to learn English?	Why do some people snore?
Why do butterflies have such colourful wings?	Why do letters in a mirror go backwards?	Why are there so many languages in the world?

BOAT to SHIP	EASY to HARD
WARM to COLD	RAIN to FALL
DOG to CAT	SIX to TEN
FOOD to MEAT	SNOW to DROP
FACE to NOSE	CHAT to CLAP
RIDE to BIKE	CAR to BUS

STOP	NILE
READ	CARE
RAMP	PLUM
STRAP	LAMP
STONE	POEM
MILE	RATS

water	wall
hair	ball
pen	dog
book	banana
hat	flower
photo	CD

telephone	ball	rain
card	door	money
book	water	road
piano	brush	tooth
apple	grass	tree
fire	chain	shirt

After the **food**, everything was washed away.

FLOOD

She liked to have a **bat** every day.

BATH

Remember to **stain** the pasta before you serve it.

STRAIN

A former runner won the Nobel **pace** prize today.

PEACE

She asked him round for a **hat**.

CHAT

The **planes** go round the sun.

PLANETS

She told him to **dive** home carefully.

DRIVE

We do not welcome idle **treats**, they said.

THREATS

They promised to enjoy the rest of their **lies** together.

LIVES

They protested against the **lad** being taken from them.

LAND

The manager said the defence has been sold all season.

SOLID

She **liked** her fingers after the meal.

LICKED

watch	telephone
shark	ant
cup	hat
rose	butter
monkey	ring
ear	fork

high	cold	fast
wet	sweet	long
happy	simple	deep
good	strong	little
big	right	dark
short	hard	dirty

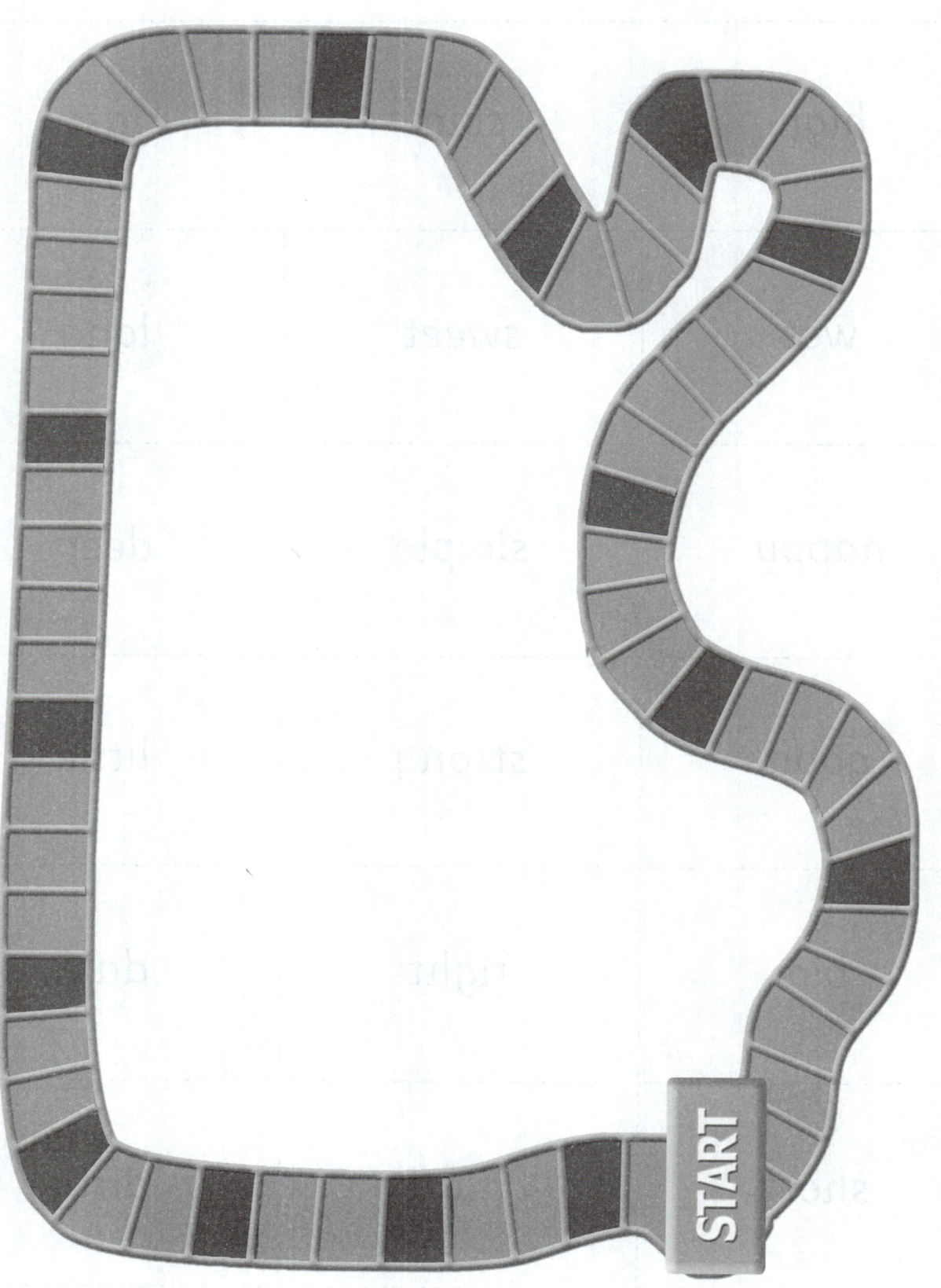

rain	rose	buttons
cars	teeth	space
England	music	fire
shoes	hair	Switzerland
butterflies	metal	dogs
money	homes	Egypt

Donald Duck	Laura Croft
Queen Elizabeth	William Shakespeare
Bill Gates	Mick Jagger
mobile phone	teddy bear
umbrella	fridge
bicycle	passport

What about Friday night then?	See you outside at 8 then.
That really wasn't necessary now, was it?	You really don't get it, do you?
I reckon that would be about right.	I just went through the roof!
Hurry up! It starts in ten minutes.	It went like a dream.
That's the third time this week. It really is too much!	So. Who is she?
Fine, thanks.	Mickey? What are you doing?

flood

It was awful. Everything indoors got wet so fast we couldn't stop **it**.

exam

I couldn't believe how easy **it** was. I knew all the answers.

headache

I've already taken two, but **it** still won't go away.

printer

Well, **it** was working an hour ago. I suppose **it**'s jammed again.

fire

They managed to put **it** out quickly and fortunately no one was hurt.

door

He tried to open **it**, but then just kicked **it** in.

sculpture

It was all twisted. I couldn't understand what **it** was supposed to be.

wedding

It was great. She looked really beautiful and everybody had a wonderful time.

car crash

It looked really nasty but they walked away with just a few cuts – nothing serious.

mirror

It just broke into pieces when I accidentally dropped **it**. Sorry if **it** was expensive.

concert

Not what I'd hoped **it** would be like. They were only on for an hour and didn't play any of their old stuff.

escaped snake

It could be anywhere now. These things can move quite fast if they want to.

cave	rope	helicopter
waterfall	fire	canoe
knife	panther	water
insects	gorilla	clothes
tent	crocodile	path
tree	rain	snake

Start

Start

Start

Start

Order a taxi.
Taxis R US

Make a dental
appointment.
Dr White

Invite to a party.
John

Order a pizza.
House of Pizza

Book a flight to Rome.
Fast Jet

Book a room.
Mirage Hotel

Order flowers for
a sick friend.
Flower shop

Change an arranged
meeting with a friend.
Marty

Arrange for your car
to be serviced.
Joe's Garage

Order a birthday cake.
The cake shop

Arrange a bank loan.
Bank Manager

Complain about some
shoes you bought.
Shoe Shop

Taxis R US	House of Pizza
John	Dr White - Dentist
Fast Let	Mirage Hotel
Flower Shop	Marty
Joe's Garage	The Cake Shop
Bank Manager	Shoe Shop

You want to live in the city centre, but your roommate wants to live in the suburbs.
(Find out why.)

Your friend borrowed your car and scratched it badly.
(You want to know how and what they are going to do about it.)

Your flatmate refuses to do any housework, claiming you do it far better.
(You want it to be shared equally.)

Your boss refuses to give you a rise this year.
(You want to know why.)

Your best friend did not ring you on your birthday.
(You want to know why.)

Your best friend went to a party without you.
(You want to know why.)

You said your friend could stay in your flat for two nights, but s/he is still there after three weeks.
(You want him/her to move out!)

You are camping and find a strange person in your tent!
(You want to know what they are doing there.)

Your parents won't let you go on holiday with your friends.
(You want to persuade them to let you.)

Your friend didn't meet you outside the cinema.
(You want to find out why.)

Your parents don't want you to move away to study at university.
(Find out why.)

Your coach hasn't let you play many games this season.
(Find out why.)

+	+	+	+
+	+	+	+
+	+	+	+
—	—	—	—
—	—	—	—
—	—	—	—

I didn't think much of the meat.	Do you fancy a coffee?
I'd like to withdraw some money, please.	Shall we go to the cinema?
Politicians are only in it for themselves.	People who live in cold countries work harder.
I don't really want to go to John's party tonight.	What do you think? Shall we eat out tonight?
I think this is the best one to get.	Does this colour suit me?
I'm going to the shop. Do you want anything?	I don't think this really suits me.

You visit the dentist after a long time.	Your flatmate has not paid her share of the rent for 6 months.
You have just returned from an awful holiday and your friend asks you about it.	You didn't go to school yesterday and the teacher wants to know why.
You have an accident in your car and report it to the police.	A policeman stops you when you are riding your motorbike.
You have a job interview.	A UFO lands in front of your house and an alien gets out.
Your best friend doesn't want to see you any more.	You want your parents to buy you a motorbike for your 17th birthday.
Your parents find something you hid in your room.	You are 14 years old. Your friend has lost your favourite CD.

Original Position	Final Position
1	1
2	2
3	3
4	4
5	5
6	6

postman	gardener
bus driver	detective
electrician	teacher
artist	actress
baker	waitress
accountant	footballer

flower	camera
hammer	paint
earring	drum
gloves	bag
torch	rope
bucket	book

START

START

START

START

(A) sandwich vs hamburger (B)	(A) football vs basketball (B)	(A) summer vs winter (B)
(A) train vs bus (B)	(A) letters vs e-mail (B)	(A) fried vs boiled (B)
(A) swimming pool vs the sea (B)	(A) glasses vs contact lenses (B)	(A) lemonade vs orange juice (B)
(A) pencil vs pen (B)	(A) classical music vs pop music (B)	(A) cassette vs CD (B)
(A) coffee vs tea (B)	(A) bicycle vs motorcycle (B)	(A) theatre vs cinema (B)
(A) newspaper vs television (B)	(A) spring vs autumn (B)	(A) cat vs dog (B)

clothes	food
books	films
flowers	festivals
cars	countries
colours	animals
sports	cities

HEART	PEPPER	SNAKE	VOLCANO
DIAMOND	SUNSET	FOREST	OCEAN
BUTTERFLY	SONG	BIG	PEBBLE
CAVE	LOST	LONG	BRIDGE
RABBIT	FRIDAY	SHOE	BELL
PIRATE	HOME	WHITE	SHARK
MOON	STAR	BRIGHT	RED
CANOE	KEY	BRONZE	ROSE
BIRD	ANT	DOLPHIN	GLASS

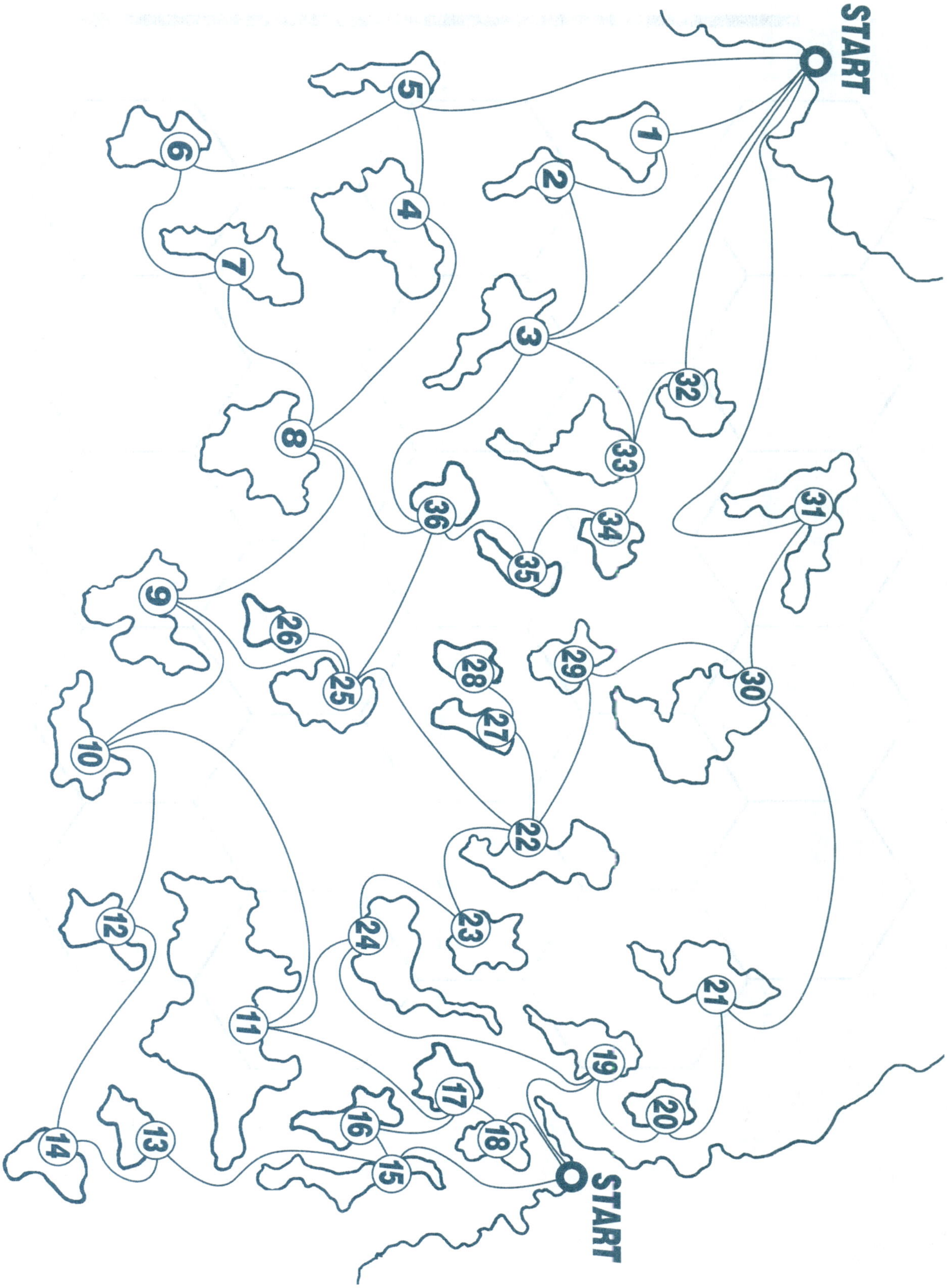

START

5
6
1
2
4
7
3
32
8
33
36
34
35
31
9
26
28
29
25
27
30
10
22
12
23
24
21
11
17
19
16
14
13
15
18
20
START

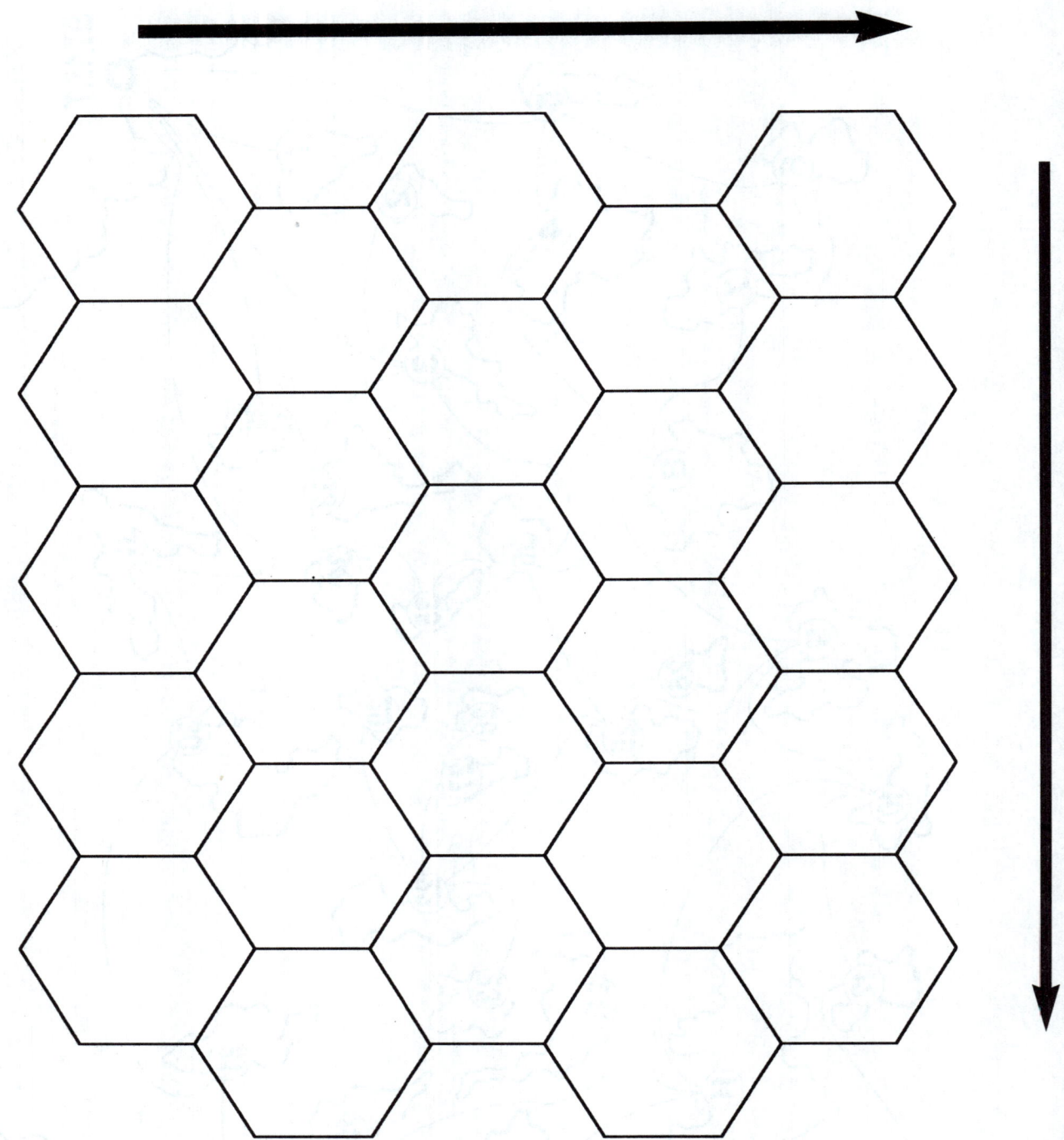

WET	DRY	TALL	SHORT
LAUGH	CRY	BRIGHT	DARK
STRONG	WEAK	SERIOUS	SILLY
HAPPY	SAD	NEAT	UNTIDY
BEGIN	END	LARGE	TINY
SWEET	SOUR	YOUNG	OLD

MOUSE	WATER
SMILE	CHOICE
RUBBISH	LUNCH
STEEL	FLOWER
JOB	DREAM
TOP	MONEY

START

HOME

FURNITURE	MUSIC
FOOD	CLOTHING
SPORTS	COUNTRIES
GEOGRAPHY	FILMS
CITIES	CELEBRATIONS
FAMOUS PEOPLE	MEANS OF TRANSPORT

 PHOTOCOPIABLE

CON	EA	AIR	INK
ATE	DE	RE	ANT
EA	PR	ARE	ED
SH	CH	OU	ETE
TH	ABLE	PRE	AY
ION	UN	OW	ISE

BREAK	HEAD
CALL	WORK
BOOK	PAY
GROW	CLOSE
CUT	LIFE
FRIEND	LIVE

LIKE	THINK
HAPPY	TELL
BELIEVE	COUNT
LOOK	SURE
ACT	TURN
AGREE	TAKE

OUS	DIS	LY	DE
ABLE	CON	NESS	CON
FUL	UN	ITY	MIS
LESS	IM	TAKE	EN
ATION	OVER	IFY	IN
MENT	UNDER	ING	PRE

1	2	3	4	5	6

	1	2	3	4	5
A					
B					
C					
D					
E					
F					
G					
H					
I					
M					
N					
R					
S					
T					

FORK *food lifter*	**ELECTRICITY** *light giver*
FOOD *stomach filler*	**CAR** *gas guzzler*
BABY *cot screamer*	**HAIR** *head warmer*
GLUE *paper sticker*	**BAG** *book carrier*
SUN *heat provider*	**ICE** *drink cooler*
CAT *rat catcher*	**SHOE** *foot supporter*

1 - P	CAPTAIN	1 - P	LIFEGUARD	1 - P	LANE
2 - O	POT	2 - O	PIN	2 - O	HOOK
3 - A	TICKLE	3 - A	EXPLAIN	3 - A	WAVE
4 - Q	FURRY	4 - Q	BRIGHT	4 - Q	HELPFUL

1 - P	ANT	1 - P	ROME	1 - P	ELF
2 - O	BOX	2 - O	LAMP	2 - O	KEY
3 - A	ARGUE	3 - A	JUMP	3 - A	KISS
4 - Q	GENTLE	4 - Q	LIFE	4 - Q	AMOUNT

1 - P	BABY	1 - P	PARROT	1 - P	THIEF
2 - O	WINDOW	2 - O	VIOLIN	2 - O	SCARF
3 - A	FALL	3 - A	GRAB	3 - A	PROMISE
4 - Q	JOY	4 - Q	TASTY	4 - Q	TRUTH

1 - P	GIANT	1 - P	HOME	1 - P	PAVEMENT
2 - O	SHELF	2 - O	DIAMOND	2 - O	COMB
3 - A	EXTEND	3 - A	ACCELERATE	3 - A	RAISE
4 - Q	TIDY	4 - Q	POOR	4 - Q	WISE

1 - P	ATTIC	1 - P	DANCER	1 - P	SHED
2 - O	MUG	2 - O	LEAF	2 - O	ORANGE
3 - A	TEAR	3 - A	RIGHT	3 - A	GROW
4 - Q	OLD	4 - Q	TRUTH	4 - Q	TOLERANT

1 - P	MANAGER	1 - P	POET	1 - P	CORNER
2 - O	TOE	2 - O	PLATE	2 - O	BUTTON
3 - A	RUB	3 - A	BOIL	3 - A	SQUEEZE
4 - Q	COOL	4 - Q	SAD	4 - Q	SMOOTH

BRIGHT LIGHT SUN DULL CLEVER	**MAP** DIRECTIONS GUIDE CHART PLACES	**FISH** NET CATCH SEA RIVER	**SATURDAY** WEEK DAY REST WORK
HUMAN ANIMAL PEOPLE WE BEING	**EARTH** PLANET MOON SPACE WORLD	**BANK** MONEY LOAN RIVER CASH	**EXAM** TEST SCHOOL MARK WRITE
PENCIL DRAW PEN PAPER WRITE	**COME** ARRIVE GO HERE TO	**CRY** TEAR SAD UNHAPPY EYE	**LEGS** ARMS BODY FEET WALK
BOOT SHOE FEET SOCK LEATHER	**DOCTOR** JOB NURSE ILL WORK	**DICTIONARY** WORDS BOOK MEAN LIST	**HISTORY** OVER GONE PAST NOW
CANDLE LIGHT WAX FIRE HEAT	**LEAF** TREE GREEN PAPER GROW	**PALACE** KING QUEEN LIVE CASTLE	**ROCK** MUSIC STONE HARD ROLL
SLEEP AWAKE EYES NIGHT BED	**CHILD** YOUNG BABY ADULT TEEN	**HAIR** COMB CUT HEAD DYE	**BOAT** WATER FISH SEA SHIP

NAME-MALE	NAME-FEMALE	COUNTRY	THINGS IN THE HOME	PLANT	ANIMAL	JOB

FIND	RELEVANT	EXAMPLES
FOLLOW	COMPLEX	PROCEDURES
GIVE	SOUND	ADVICE
TAKE	APPROPRIATE	ACTION
MAKE	SERIOUS	MISTAKE
HOLD	STRONG	OPINION

5 countries beginning with A	5 types of furniture
5 facial expressions	5 means of transport
5 outdoor jobs	5 wild animals
5 types of jewellery	5 girls' names with one syllable
5 activities you can do in the sea	5 good qualities
5 vegetarian foods	5 bad habits

short	closely
kind	long
happily	brightly
lived	guarded
hearted	winded
married	painted

A poor boy went to market to sell the family cow.

The light came on suddenly...

Yesterday was the happiest day of my life.

He thought he had a job for life, but ...

The world had changed completely.

My friend Peter liked to help other people.

Sam was my pet ...

Once upon a time, there was a ...

He should never have answered the telephone that day.

If only she had stayed at home that day ...

It was a dark and stormy night ...

As I was walking down the street, ...

Your friend's mother offers you some food which you never eat. What would you do?
A Say thank you and eat it.
B Say you have a sudden stomach ache
C Accept it but do not touch it.

Your friend buys you a ticket to go together to a film. You have seen the film and thought it was really boring. What would you say?
A Thanks but I don't want to see it.
B Why didn't you ask me first if I wanted to go?
C Great! Let's go.

You invite friends for dinner but find you don't have time to cook. What would you do?
A Order take-away.
B Phone them and cancel the evening.
C Suggest eating out when they arrive.

You wake up two hours late for school. What would you do?
A Go to school and apologise to the teacher.
B Phone the secretary and say you are ill.
C Turn over and go back to sleep.

Your friend gives you an expensive book as a present, but you already have it. What would you do?
A Say thank you and secretly go to the shop to change it.
B Save it to give to another friend as a birthday present.
C Thank your friend but say you already have it.

It is raining heavily and a passing bus soaks your clothes with dirty water. You are already late for an important meeting. What would you do?
A Go home and change.
B Go to the meeting anyway.
C Phone and cancel.

You find a little puppy outside your house. What would you do?
A Leave it.
B Take it home
C Try to sell it.

You break your best friend's valuable camera. What would you do?
A Tell your friend and apologise.
B Pretend you don't know anything about it.
C Say it was stolen.

Your best friend forgets your birthday. What would you do?
A Call them and say how upset you are.
B Say nothing.
C Deliberately forget their birthday.

You accidentally see the questions for an exam that your class is going to take on your teacher's desk. What do you do?
A Tell all the class what the questions are.
B Tell nobody.
C Tell the teacher so they can change the exam.

A relative gives you a present of a lot of money. What do you do with it?
A Put most of it in the bank.
B Spend most of it on yourself.
C Give most of it to charity.

There is only one piece of some delicious food left on a plate in the middle of the table. What do you do?
A Take it yourself when nobody is looking.
B Ask if anybody wants the last piece.
C Wait for somebody else to take it.

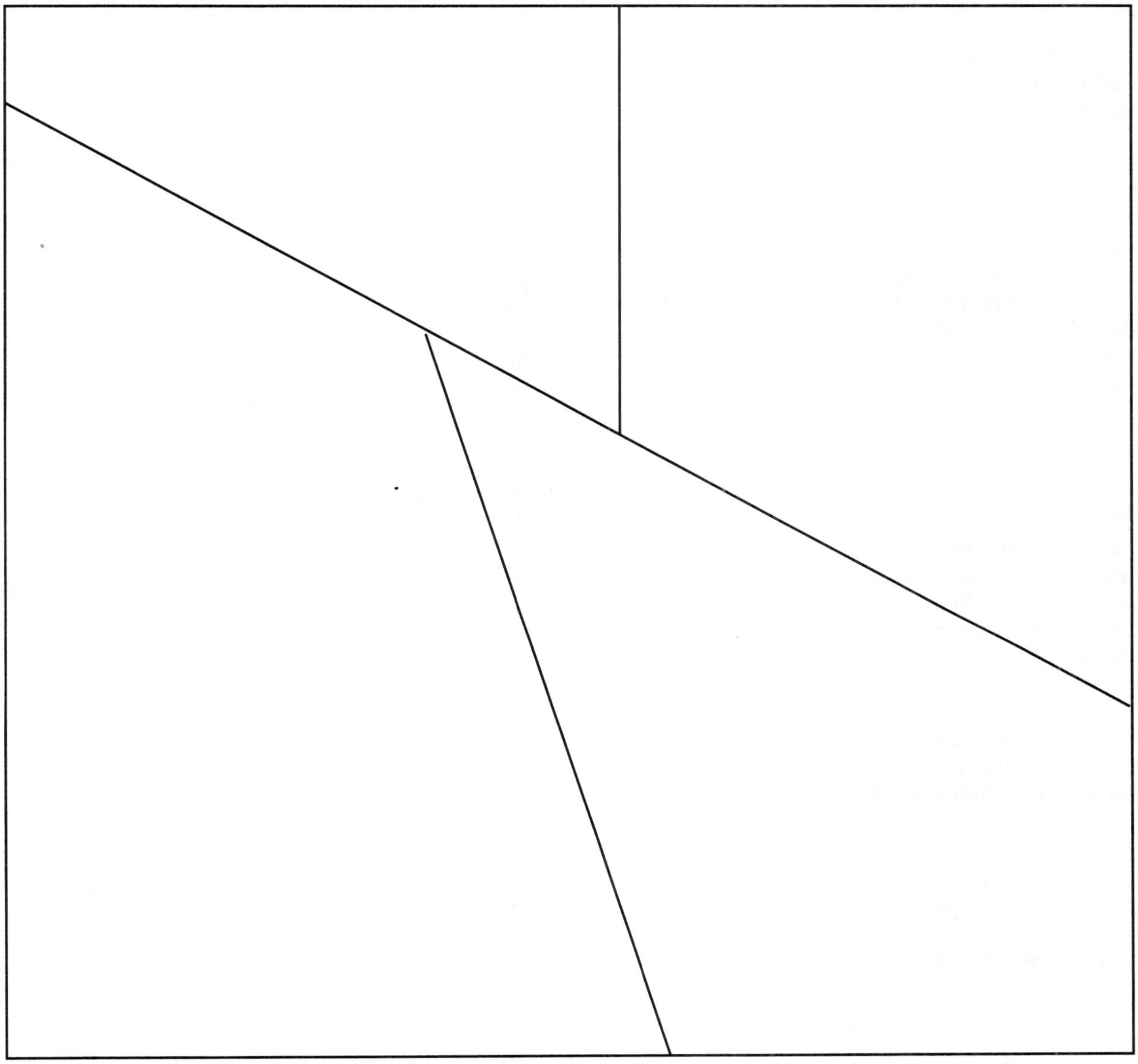

How to make a predictor

Use a square piece of paper (21cm by 21cm is a good size). Fold one corner to meet the other and make a sharp crease. Open the paper and make a crease with the other corners.

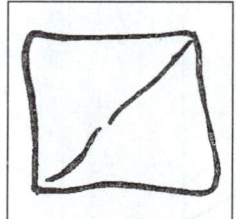 

Take one corner and fold it to the centre and make a sharp crease. Do the same with the other three corners.

Keep the paper folded and turn it over. Fold one corner to the centre pressing hard to make a sharp crease. Do the same with the other three corners.

  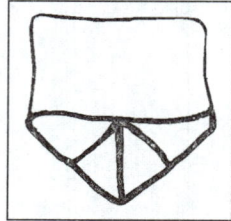 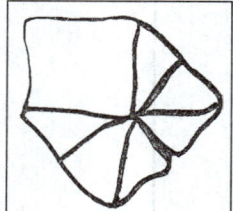

Fold the square in half so that the flaps are on the outside making sure to press hard on the crease. Open it and fold it the other way.

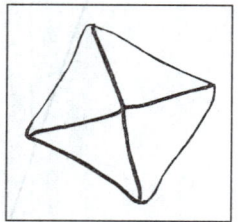  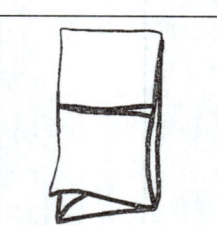

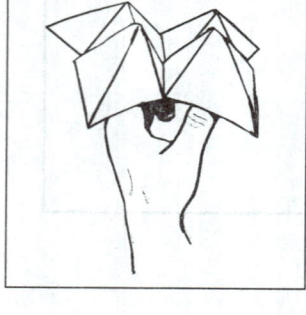

Put your fingers under the flaps and practise opening and closing your predictor.

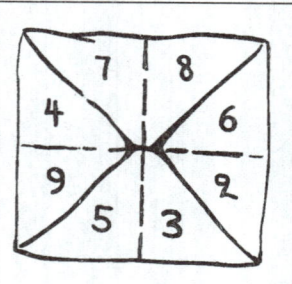

Open the predictor and write numbers on the inside flaps.

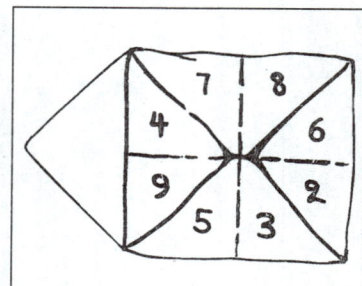

Open each flap and *under* the flaps write a prediction or prompts for whatever language area you are practising.

It was a dark and stormy night.

When in doubt, panic!

The best food is cooked at home.

I saw him last night.

All that glitters is not gold.

A man is known by the company he keeps.

To be or not to be, that is the question.

Life is not a bowl of cherries.

People in glass houses should not throw stones.

We sat round the fire talking.

Never say never.

When a man is tired of London, he is tired of life.

PHOTOCOPIABLE

I am liking taking holidays. I like taking holidays.	Many mens do this. Many men do this.	This photo doesn't looks like you. This photo doesn't look like you.
I always have to make the cooking. I always have to do the cooking.	The English is difficult for me. English is difficult for me.	Look the view. Look at the view.
The people who they live there are friendly. The people who live there are friendly.	Where you went yesterday? Where did you go yesterday?	I can't concentrate for my work. I can't concentrate on my work.
How was it like? What was it like?	I must to leave now. I must leave now.	I have a long time to see. I haven't seen you in a long time.
It happened the same to me. The same thing happened to me.	She is a great city. It is a great city.	I think is the best thing to do. I think it is the best thing to do.
I lost the bus this morning. I missed the bus this morning.	He has very much problems. He has very many problems.	May you open the window please? Can you open the window please?

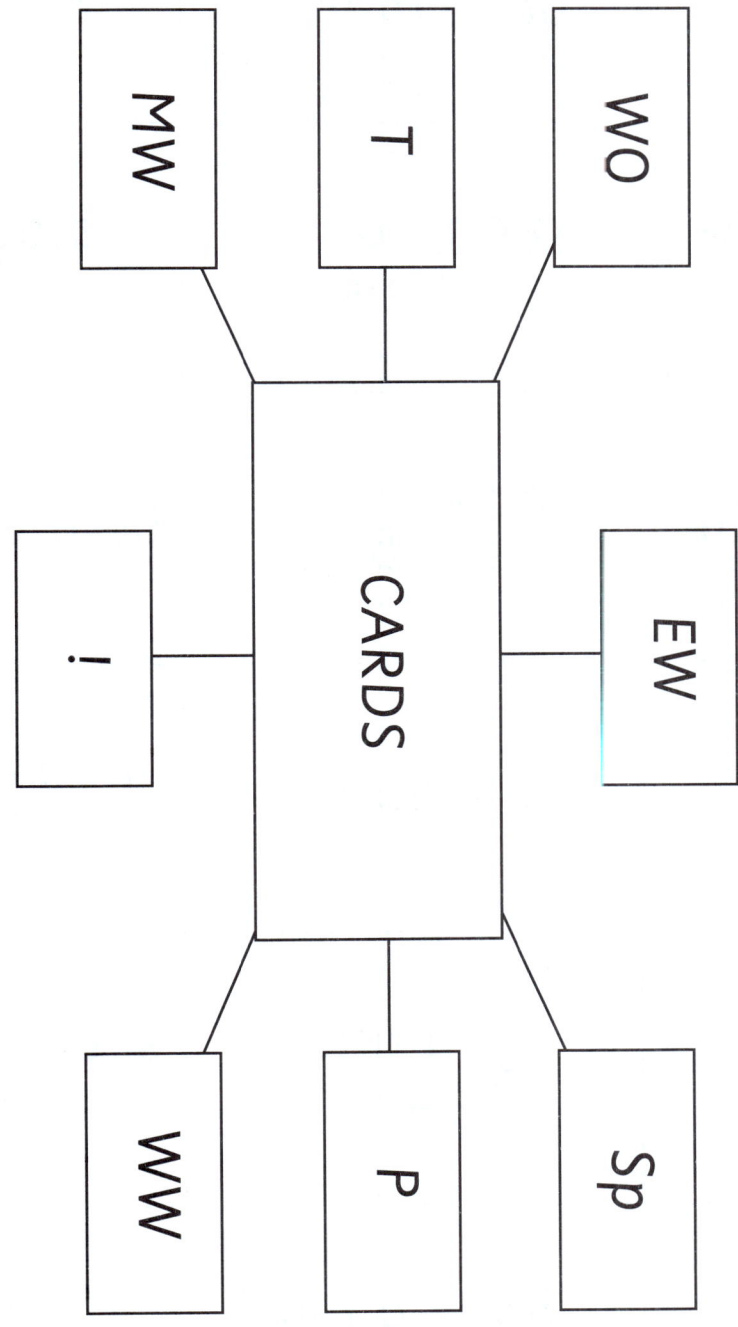

live alone	give away your money	ride a horse
live in another country	go on holiday alone	stay up all night
sing in public	paint your room black	be a vegetarian
break a promise	go camping	go swimming alone
run a marathon	go hang gliding	sail around the world
dye your hair	have a pet snake	work on a farm

-10	-9	-8	-7	-6	-5	-4	-3	-2	-1	0	1	2	3	4	5	6	7	8	9	10

Find a mechanic.

Read a book.

Stop in next town.

Call the police.

Call a doctor.

Wear more clothes.

Take the bus.

Go home.

Listen to the radio.

Stop and camp.

Eat a good meal.

Buy a sleeping bag.

Have a flat tyre.

Feel cold.

Lose map.

Get lost.

Lose pedal.

Have accident.

Tent blows away.

Lose money.

Feel lonely.

Feel hungry.

Run out of water.

Can't sleep.

You are afraid.
There is an earthquake.
You are going to hide
under the table.

You are hot.
You are sunbathing on the beach.
You are going to buy
an ice cream.

You are cold.
There is no heating in
the house.
You are going to go to bed.

You can't sleep.
You have an exam in the morning.
You are going to listen
to some relaxing music.

You can't get into your house.
You have lost your keys.
You go and stay at a friend's.

Your eyes ache.
You have been working
on the computer too long.
You are going to take a break.

You have stomach ache.
You ate some seafood that was
off.
You are going to go to bed.

You have a very bad headache.
You were at a loud rock concert
last night.
You are going to take some aspirin.

You are on the last train
home and miss your stop.
You fell asleep and you have no
money with you.
You decide to sleep on the train.

You are relieved.
You have finished your exams.
You are going to have a party.

Your mobile phone doesn't work.
It fell into the sea.
You are going to replace it.

You are very happy.
You just got a new job.
You are going to buy some new
clothes.

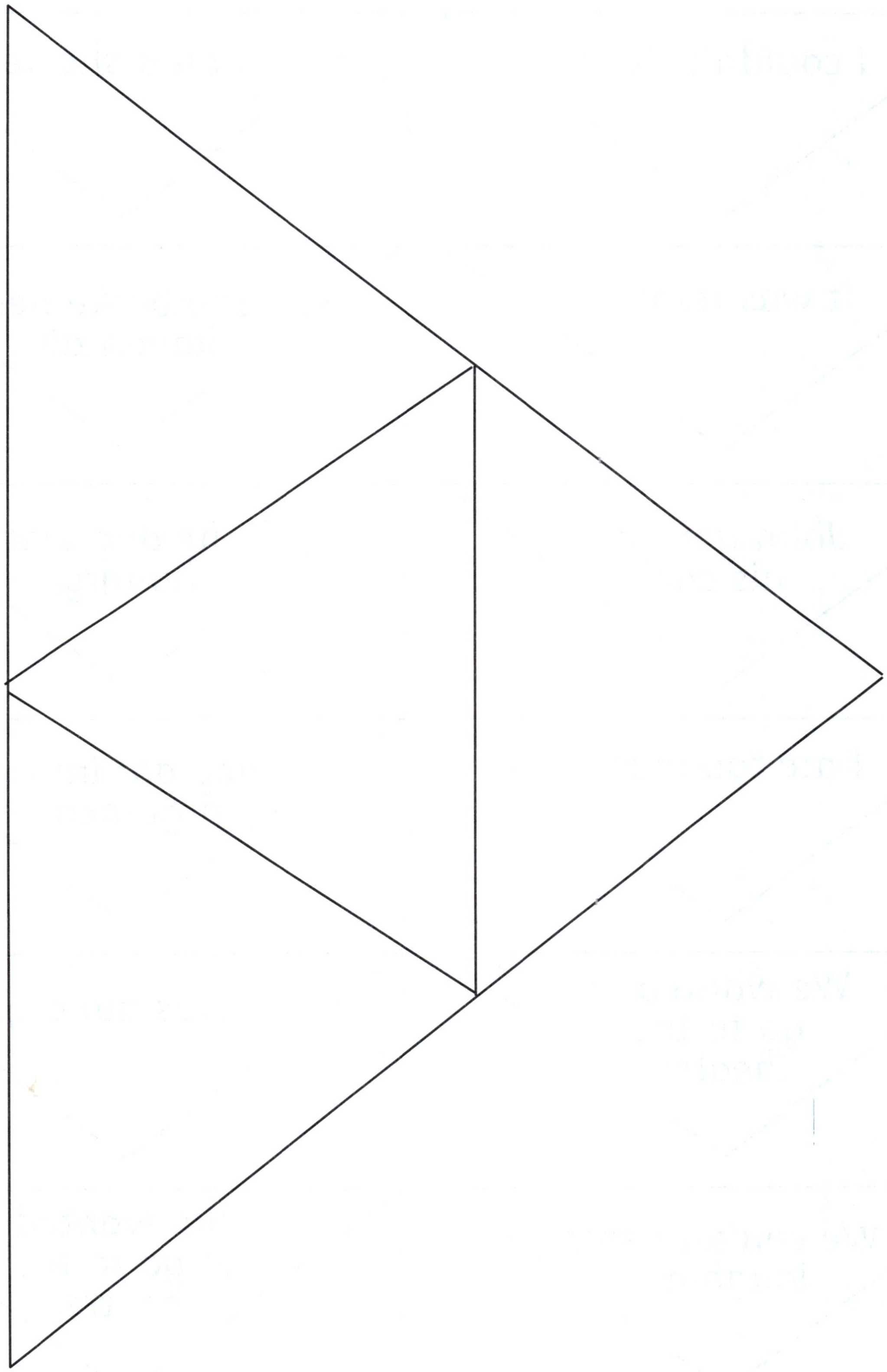

I couldn't sleep.

I had a shower.

It was raining.

She broke her fingernail.

John got into his car.

The dog was hungry.

I ate too much.

They got into an argument.

We wanted to go to the theatre.

I was hungry.

We couldn't stop laughing.

Jim wanted to go to the theatre.

so

so

so

so

but

but

but

but

and

and

and

and

I saw this amazing thing!

It must have been the wrong day.

She just said no.

Then the lights went out.

Then it all went wrong.

It was absolutely awful!

We were feeling pretty good.

I'll never do that again!

We thought we had no chance.

It was much too early for that.

I had just missed her.

It was a dream come true.

How ?	How?	How?
When?	When?	When?
Where?	Where?	Where?
Why?	Why?	Why?
Who?	Who?	Who?
What?	What?	What?

The best is yet to come.

As old as the hills.

Better to be happy than rich.

Too many cooks spoil the broth.

A stitch in time saves nine.

Laugh and the world laughs with you.

Time is money.

Every cloud has a silver lining.

Once bitten twice shy.

Give peace a chance.

To be or not to be.

You can't take it with you.

cold/old	tree/knee	go/know
top/stop	train/rain	bread/said
hair/bear	ear/here	night/fight
boat/goat	day/play	caught/thought
flood/mud	eat/feet	hour/tower
hat/cat	sad/lad	hair/where

sea/see	some/sum	write/right
toe/tow	seen/scene	been/bean
mail/male	sew/so	know/no
buy/bye	bread/bred	here/hear
lone/loan	die/dye	pane/pain
made/maid	deer/dear	fair/fare

BAT	BRED
MET	MAN
LED	PROD
LAD	HAT
WED	TRY
MAT	MAD

 PHOTOCOPIABLE

●●● ●	●●●	●●●●	●●●●	●●●●			

→		✗	✓	?		📢		↓
👂	→	📢	👂	✗		✓	↓	👂
✓	?	→	📢	👂	?	↓	?	✗
	✓	✓	→	✗	↓	👂	📢	
?	✗	?	👂	☺	✓	✓	👂	?
📢		👂	📢	?	←	✗		📢
	👂	📢	↑	📢		←	✗	
✗		↑	✗		?	✓	←	✓
📢	↑	📢	✓	?		✗	👂	←

| start ↑ | | ST - ✗ | INT - ✓ | SS - 👂 | N - 📢 | C - ? | TT - ☺ |

ST - ✗

ST - ✗

INT - ✓

INT - ✓

SS - 👂

SS - 👂

N - 📢

N - 📢

C - ?

C - ?

TT - ☺

TT - ☺

● ● / ● ●

She's having another baby. Is that true?

● ● ● / ● ●

Can I bring some friends? The more the merrier.

● ● / ● ●

Can you help me for a minute? No problem!

● ● / ● ●

Sorry I'm late. Never mind!

● ● ● / ●

How was the film? Not bad really.

● ● ● / ● ●

When will you finish it? As soon as I can.

● ● / ● ●

She's not here. Where's she gone?

● ● ● / ●

You never do anything useful around here! Give me a break!

● ● ● ● / ●

Life's very expensive these days. I know what you mean.

● ● ● / ●

I've got to go now. See you later.

● ● ● ● ● / ●

See you at 8 tonight? If I can manage it.

● ● ● / ●

The door was left unlocked last night. Don't blame me.

I told you to turn **left** at the second traffic lights. (Not right.)	Tuesday is all right with **me**. (But what about you?)	Gold **is** better than silver. (How can you doubt it?)
You actually **liked** living there? (You didn't hate it?)	The accident wasn't **my** fault. (But it was the other driver's.)	It's **true** what I'm telling you. (It is not false.)
Why don't **you** cook for a change? (I always cook.)	But what do **you** think? (I know what I think.)	Monday **could** be OK. Let me check. (I'm not sure.)
You don't believe me. (But others do.)	Well, the **price** was better than I'd expected. (But the quality wasn't.)	He really said **that**! (Not what I'd expected.)
He didn't tell **me** why. (But he told someone else.)	I can't really talk to you **now**. (But maybe later.)	The fish I caught **was** this big. (But not what you've heard.)
The **dessert** was great. (But not the main course.)	**He** liked the film. (But I didn't.)	You didn't tell her **Tuesday**, did you? (It should be another day.)

shoe	chair
tree	jam
fire	nose
lake	rain
rain	water
garden	sun

The wheels of the bus go round and round, round and round, round and round.
The wheels of the bus go round and round. All day long.
The bell on the bus goes ding, ding, ding...
The wipers of the bus go swish, swish, swish...
The windows of the bus go up and down...
The people on the bus go chat, chat,chat...
The babies on the bus go wah!, wah!, wah!...
The mummies on the bus go sh, sh, sh... etc

Head & shoulders, knees and toes, knees and toes,
Head & shoulders, knees and toes, knees and toes,
And eyes and ears and mouth and nose,
Head & shoulders, knees and toes, knees and toes!

This is the way we wash our face, wash our face, wash our face
This is the way we wash our face early in the morning!
This is the way we brush our teeth...
                we comb our hair...
                we put on our clothes...
                we tie our shoes...
                we go to school...

If you're happy and you know it, clap your hands
If you're happy and you know it, clap your hands
If you're happy and you know it, and you really want to show it
If you're happy and you know it, clap your hands
If you're happy and you know it, stamp your feet
                                snap your fingers
                                slap your thighs
                                say "we are"!
                                do all five

Incey wincey spider climbed up the water spout
Down came the rain and washed the spider out
Out came the sun and dried up all the rain
And Incey wincey spider climbed up the spout again!

Row, row, row your boat [repeat]
Gently down the stream [repeat]
Merrily, merrily, merrily, merrily [repeat]
Life is but a dream [repeat]

The best little animal's a tiny mouse
You can find it in a field, you can find it in your house
They frighten great big elephants but they don't frighten me
I often have a party and invite them in for tea

There Was an Old Woman Who Swallowed a Fly

There was an old woman who swallowed a fly,
I don't know why she swallowed a fly,
Perhaps she'll die!

There was an old woman who swallowed a spider,
That wriggled and jiggled and tickled inside her,
She swallowed the spider to catch the fly,
I don't know why she swallowed a fly,
Perhaps she'll die!

There was an old woman who swallowed a bird,
How absurd! To swallow a bird.
She swallowed the bird to catch the spider,
That wriggled and jiggled and tickled inside her,
She swallowed the spider to catch the fly,
I don't know why she swallowed a fly,
Perhaps she'll die!

There was an old woman who swallowed a cat,
Imagine that! To swallow a cat.
She swallowed the cat to catch the bird,
She swallowed the bird to catch the spider,
That wriggled and jiggled and tickled inside her,
She swallowed the spider to catch the fly,
I don't know why she swallowed a fly,
Perhaps she'll die!

There was an old woman who swallowed a dog,
Oh, what a hog! To swallow a dog.
She swallowed the dog to catch the cat,
She swallowed the cat to catch the bird,
She swallowed the bird to catch the spider,
That wriggled and jiggled and tickled inside her,
She swallowed the spider to catch the fly,
I don't know why she swallowed a fly,
Perhaps she'll die!

There was an old woman who swallowed a goat,
She opened her mouth and it went down her throat!
She swallowed the goat to catch the dog,
She swallowed the dog to catch the cat,
She swallowed the cat to catch the bird,
She swallowed the bird to catch the spider,
That wriggled and jiggled and tickled inside her,
She swallowed the spider to catch the fly,
I don't know why she swallowed a fly,
Perhaps she'll die!

There was an old woman who swallowed a cow,
I don't know how she swallowed a cow!
She swallowed the cow to catch the goat,
She swallowed the goat to catch the dog,
She swallowed the dog to catch the cat,
She swallowed the cat to catch the bird,
She swallowed the bird to catch the spider,
That wriggled and jiggled and tickled inside her,
She swallowed the spider to catch the fly,
I don't know why she swallowed a fly,
Perhaps she'll die!

There was an old woman who swallowed a horse!

She died, of course!

There Was an Old Woman Who Swallowed a Fly

There was an old woman who swallowed a fly,
I don't know why she swallowed a fly ,
Perhaps she'll die!

There was an old woman who swallowed a spider,
That wriggled and jiggled and tickled inside her,
She swallowed the spider to catch the fly,
I don't know why she swallowed a fly,
Perhaps she'll die!

There was an old woman who swallowed ....,
How absurd! To swallow ....
She swallowed the .... to catch the spider,
That wriggled and jiggled and tickled inside her,
She swallowed the spider to catch the fly,
I don't know why she swallowed a fly,
Perhaps she'll die!

There was ....,
Imagine that! ....
She .... to catch the ....,
She .... to catch the ....,
That .... her,
She swallowed the spider to catch the fly,
I don't know why she swallowed a fly,
Perhaps she'll die!

....,
Oh, what a hog! ....
She .... to ....,
....,
....,
....,
I don't know why she swallowed a fly,
Perhaps she'll die!

....,
She opened her mouth and it went down her throat!
She swallowed ....,
....,
....,
....,
....,
....,
I don't know why she swallowed a fly,
Perhaps she'll die!

....,
I don't know how .... !
....,
....,
....,
....,
....,
....,
Perhaps she'll die!

.... !

She died, of course!

 PHOTOCOPIABLE

Horror	Folk Tale
Science Fiction	Comedy
Adventure	Fantasy
It was a dark and stormy night ...	The only clue was the broken window.
Once upon a time ...	He gazed longingly out the window.
You wouldn't believe me if I told you there are little green people living in my garden.	He seemed to have everything you could hope for, but he had a dark secret.

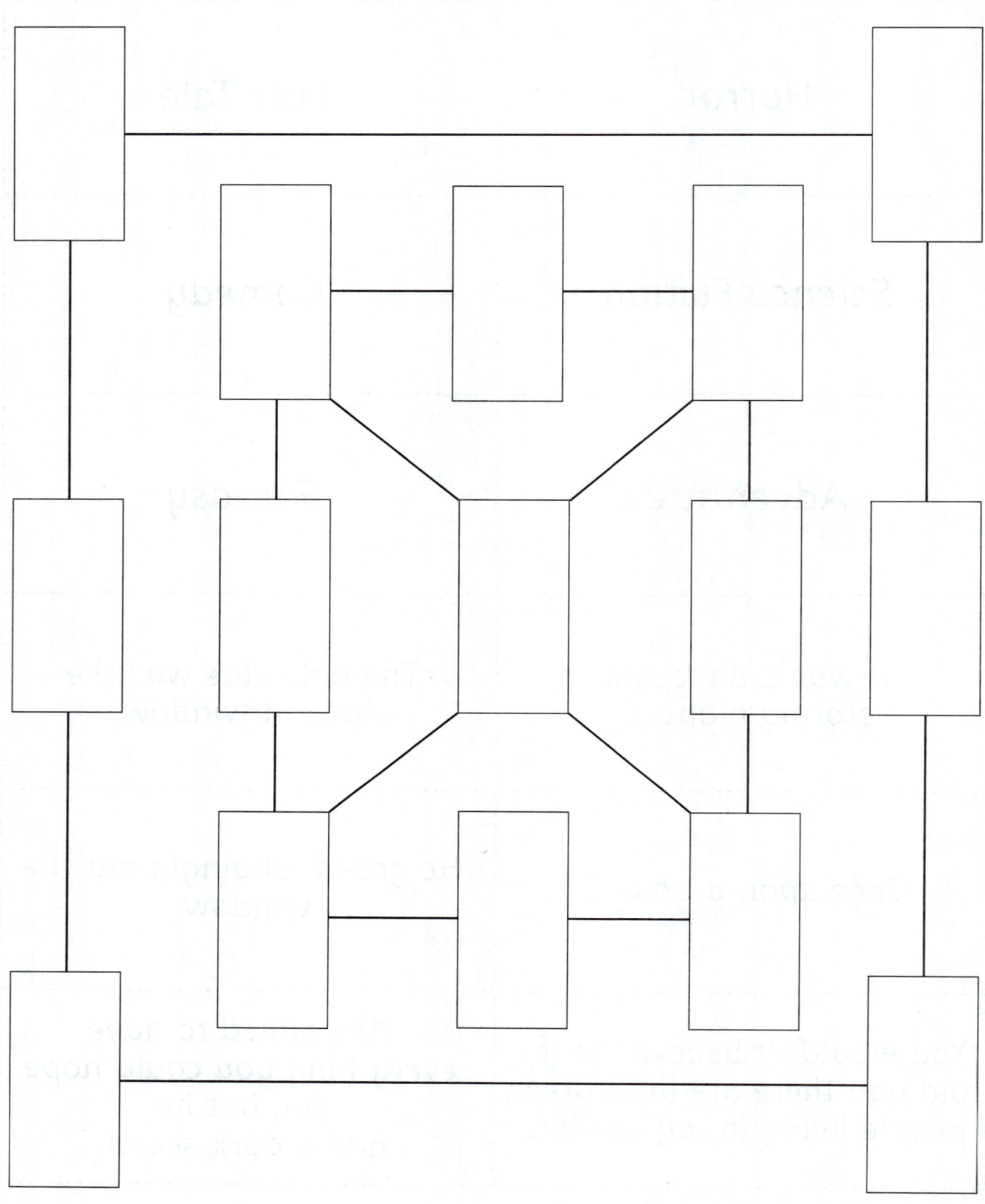

I have long time to see you.

I lost the bus.

This is not tasting nice, no?

Why wanting you this?

Never I said this!

What time do you think it is?

You're getting on my nerves!

Fancy a coffee?

If you will, I will!

We're off tomorrow.

I don't have nothing to say.

It looks like it's going to rain.

My 1st is in deck but not in peck.
My 2nd is in pick and also in sick.
My 3rd is in cold but not in hold.
My 4th is in time but not in lime.
My 5th is in will and also in fill.
My 6th is in fool and also in cool.
My 7th is in nose but not in hose.
My 8th is in hand and also in land.
My 9th is in red but not in fed.
My 10th is in yet but not in net.
What am I?

My 1st is in crash but not in smash.
My 2nd is in crack but not in smack.
My 3rd is in broke and also in smoke.
My 4th is in kick but not in sink.
My 5th is in grow and also in show.
My 6th is in made but not in make.
My 7th is in fill and also in will.
My 8th is in life but not in wife.
My 9th is in Eve but not in Adam.
What am I?

My 1st is in carry but not in marry.
My 2nd is in four and also in tour.
My 3rd is in map but not in lap.
My 4th is in jump and also in pump.
My 5th is in sum and also in mum.
My 6th is in take but not in wake.
My 7th is in set and also in net.
My 8th is in reach but not in peach.
What am I?

My 1st is in boat but not in coat.
My 2nd is in light and also in fight.
My 3rd is in cat but not in mat.
My 4th is in ray and also in say.
My 5th is in catch and also in match.
My 6th is in look but not in book
My 7th is in pen and also in hen.
What am I?

My 1st is in mist and also in fist.
My 2nd is in sun but not in fun.
My 3rd is in land but not in hand.
My 4th is in hall and also in wall.
My 5th is in song and also in long.
My 6th is in date but not in late.
What am I?

My 1st is in fish but not in dish.
My 2nd is in read but not in bead.
My 3rd is in lick and also in kick.
My 4th is in egg and also in leg.
My 5th is in now but not in cow.
My 6th is in dam but not in ram.
What am I?

1	2	3
4	5	6
7	8	9
10		

 **Game On**

1

2

3

4

5

6

7

8

9

10

  PHOTOCOPIABLE

1	2	3
4	5	6
7	8	9
10		

A	A	A	A	A	A
A	A	A	B	B	B

C	C	C

D	D	D	D

E	E	E	E	E	E
E	E	E	E	E	E

F	F	G	G	G

H	H	H

I	I	I	I	I	I
I	I	I	J	K	
L	L	L	L	M	M
N	N	N	N	N	N
O	O	O	O	O	O
O	O				
P	P				
Q					

 PHOTOCOPIABLE

R R R R R R

S S S S S S

T T T T T T

U U U U

V V

W W

X Y Y Y

Z

FINISH

START